Easy Needle Felting Guide: Learn From Scratch

Tai .B Palacios

Funny helpful tips:

Practice vulnerability; it deepens emotional connection.

Stay authentic; genuine interactions build trust and rapport.

Easy Needle Felting Guide: Learn From Scratch : Unlock the Art of Needle Felting with a Step-by-Step Guide for Beginners

Life advices:

Engage with books that promote critical thinking; they equip you to evaluate information in an age of information overload.

Stay vigilant about deepfake technology; its ability to manipulate media poses challenges for authenticity verification.

Introduction

This book provides a creative and hands-on introduction to the art of needle felting, allowing individuals to create beautiful and unique felted projects. This guide offers a variety of projects and techniques to get you started in this craft.

The guide features a range of projects, including a charming needle-felted llama ornament, a cute yellow-eyed penguin Christmas tree decoration, and a proposal pillow, each with step-by-step instructions for crafting your own felted masterpiece. It also outlines the necessary supplies for these projects, making it easy for beginners to gather what they need.

Realistic animal needle felting techniques are explored in detail, providing readers with insights into creating lifelike felted animals. The guide covers the fundamentals of needle felting, explaining the essential tools and materials required to get started in this craft.

Additionally, readers can learn how to create felted stripe Christmas stockings, with a list of necessary supplies and clear step-by-step directions to follow. The guide ensures that individuals have a solid understanding of the basics of needle felting, setting them on the path to successfully create their own felted projects.

This book is a comprehensive resource that equips readers with the knowledge and skills needed to explore the world of needle felting. Whether you're interested in crafting festive ornaments or realistic animal sculptures, this guide provides the guidance and inspiration to bring your felted creations to life.

Contents

CHAPTER ONE

Introduction

Felting with a Needle

In a nutshell, needle felting is the technique of changing wool into three-dimensional objects with the help of a barbed needle. In this guide I will be revealing to you DIY step by step guide on how to needle felt different kind of teddy bear/dolls, Christmas hats, birds and animals, Santa and an additional project on proposal pillow!

When you felt wool, you agitate the fibers, causing them to fuse together and form a solid cloth. If you've ever felted a knitting project, you're already familiar with the procedure, only you presumably used a washing machine with really hot water to attach the fibers. Needle felting is similar to that procedure, except instead of churning the wool with hot water, you use an extra-sharp needle.

CHAPTER TWO

Needle-Felted Llama Ornament DIY

This fluffy white llama is handcrafted of soft felted roving, has a lavishly embroidered saddle blanket, and a sleeping smile that charms both youngsters and adults.

This is a suggestion from a buddy. Her adorable friend is needle-felted. This method entails sculpting shapes from unspun wool roving by manipulating the strands with a specific needle until they interlock and become thick. One of these llamas may be made in roughly an hour by an experienced artisan. The biggest difference between this project and our other needle-felted animals is that you will skip the pipe-cleaner armature step because this llama is intended to hang from the branches of your Christmas tree.

This will necessitate the use of tools and supplies.

• roving in white felt

• Snips for fine details

• Needle for embroidery

• Embroidery floss in black

• Gold embroidery thread

• Embroidery thread

• Felt roving in various colors for saddle blanket

• Felting pad

• Felting using needles

• Ribbon and appliqué embellishment

• Gold, light

• Glue for crafts

How to Go About It(Procedures)

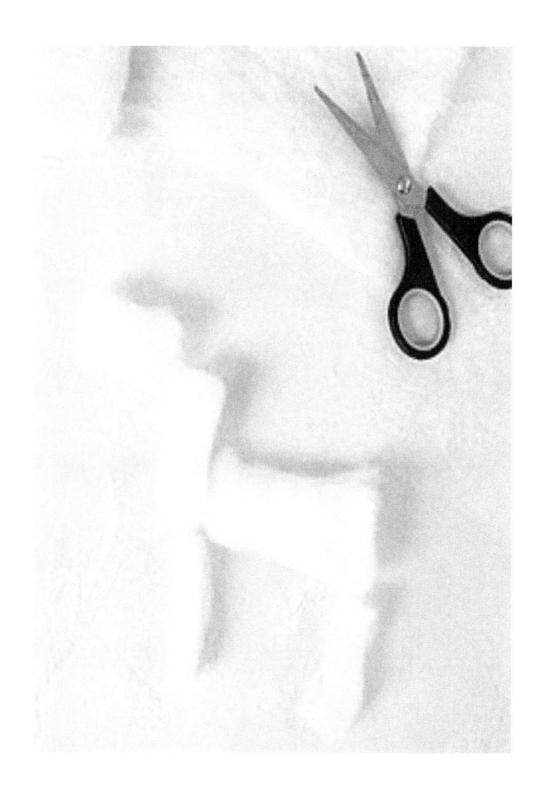

STEP ONE: Take a huge amount of white roving and pinch out smaller pieces to allot for different llama body parts as illustrated.

(Note: Don't be concerned if your llama appears overly large; the wool roving will shrink in size as you needle-felt it.) For reference, our pre-felted llama was 6 inches broad and 4 inches tall.)

NEXT STEP: Place roving on a needle-felting mat for each body part; punch the fibers all over with a needle-felting tool, manipulating the roving with your fingers as you work, until they feel dense and firm. (Tip: Always make sure your needle is facing straight down and not at an angle, since this might cause it to break.)

3RD STEP: Assemble the llama: Join the head, neck, and limbs to the body by pounding the fibers with the tool and, if required, using a bit of extra roving.

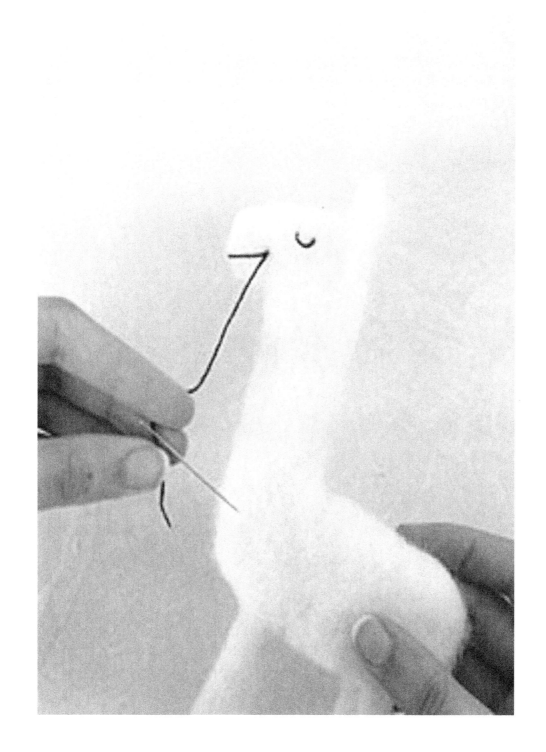

4th STEP: Add the following facial traits to the llama: Thread a needle with black embroidery floss and tie one end; enter the needle through the snout and wrap around the opposite side; knot the other end. To embroider eyes, use stem stitch on a little diagonal, making all visible stitches the same length.

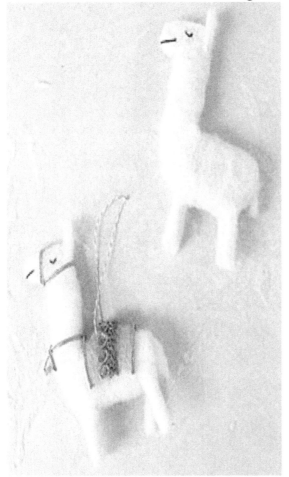

5th STEP: Add the following accessories to the llama: Cut a square sheet of pink roving, decorate with beautiful trim, and drape over the back of the llama. Make a harness by wrapping gold embroidery floss around the snout and neck. Then, for hanging, thread a loop of embroidery floss through the llama's back and tie the ends into a knot.

CHAPTER THREE

Yellow-eyed Penguin Christmas Tree Decoration (Do-It-Yourself)

Every year, I make a new bird ornament for our Christmas tree. The trouble is that I generally get preoccupied and forget about them, so you'll occasionally discover the remains of long-forgotten decorations scattered across my workplace. kkp torso! Open a drawer! Open a cabinet — that was supposed to be a kkriki crown!

Because the hoiho (yellow-eyed penguin) was named Bird of the Year this year, I was inspired to complete an ornament for our Christmas tree. I even took photos along the route and developed a design off of them.

There's still room for experimentation. You could replace the Santa hat with a crown, or leave the bottom open and place it on top of your tree (since, let's face it, the hoiho is an angel).

I'm also working on a simpler version for kids (which will be available shortly). Instead of a blanket stitch, it employs hot glue.

Supplies are required.

- 1 black (or dark grey) felt sheet

- 1 yellow felt sheet

- 1 piece of white felt

- 1 pink, orange, or light brown felt sheet

- 1 red felt sheet

- Cotton stranded in black

- Cotton stranded in white

- Cotton stranded in silver or gold

- A hot glue gun (with glue)

- Filling a hobby

Extras available as options:

- Googly or crystal eyes (instead of felt)

- Folley bell(s) for added holiday jingle

Step 1: Print the pattern and cut it out.

Print the pattern on an A4 sheet of paper and cut the parts out.

This will result in a decoration 11.5 centimetres (4.5 inches) tall.

Attachments

Step 2: Cut the Felt Into Pieces

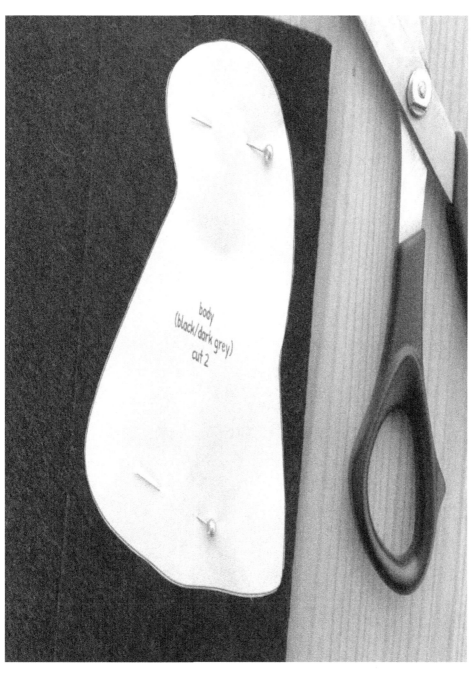

Arrange the pattern pieces on the felt. Before cutting out the patterns, use pins to support them.

Some sections must be cut on the fold of the fabric (see photos).

If you need to cut two pieces, I found that folding the cloth and cutting the pieces at the same time was easier. This resulted in a more consistent cut while also saving money on cloth.

Step 3: Attach the Tummy Pieces to the Body Pieces using Glue.

Before gluing, set the tummy parts on the body pieces and try putting the body pieces together to see that everything is centered correctly.

When you're satisfied, run your hot glue gun along the edges of the tummy pieces and stick them to the body pieces.

I tried putting these on after I'd sewn the body sections together, but it resulted in the tummy pieces looking crinkled.

Step 4: Sew the Middle Piece to the Body Piece's Back.

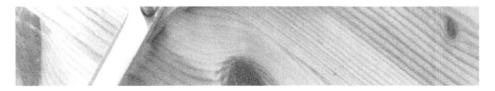

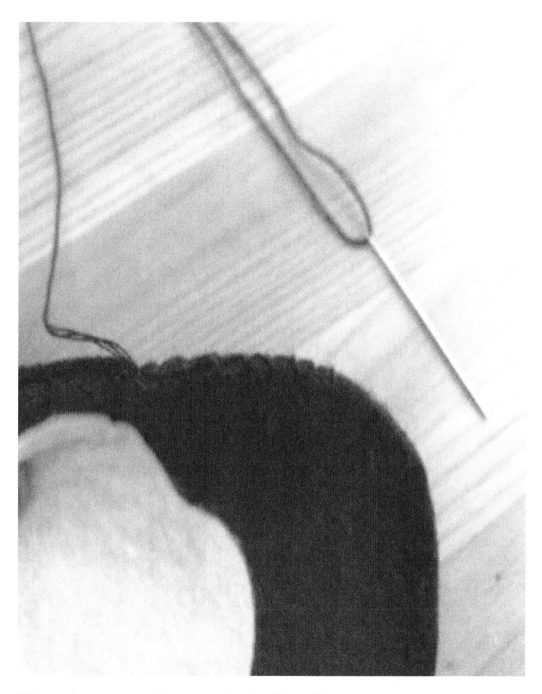

Place the center piece on the inside of the body piece. It should be able to accommodate the penguin's head's curve (see photos for an

example).

To attach the pieces, use a blanket stitch.

Step 5: Sew the Middle Piece to the Body Piece's Bottom.

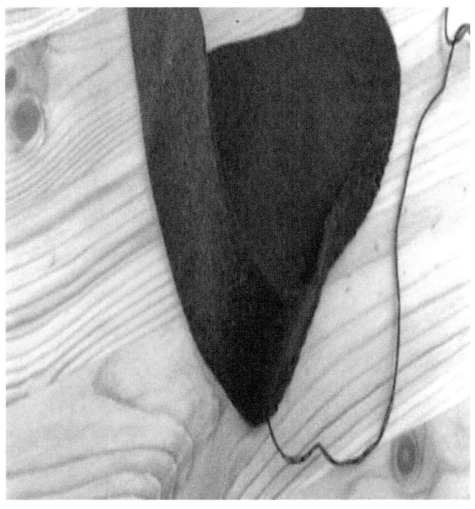

When you reach the end of the lined-up pieces, curve the center piece so it lines up with the bottom of the body piece (see photos). To attach the pieces, use a blanket stitch.

Try to feed the needle between the layers once you've struck places with the white tummy piece (see photo).

Sew the Middle Piece Along the Front of the Body Piece (Step 6).

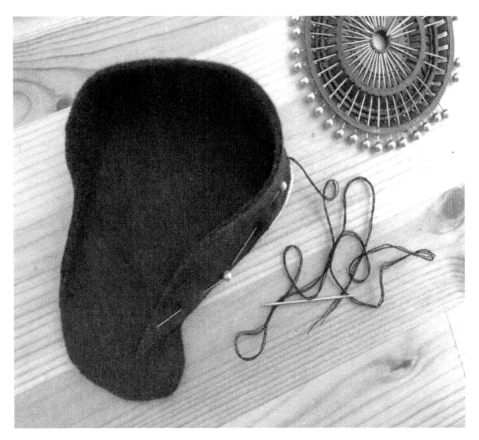

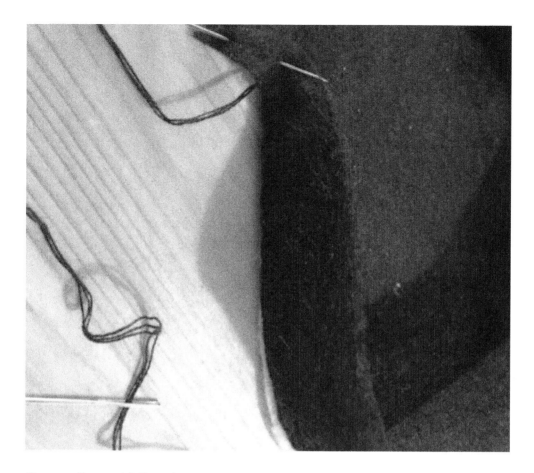

Curve the middle piece once more so that it aligns with the front of the body piece (see photos).

To attach the pieces, use a blanket stitch.

Keep in mind that there is one small part at the end of the middle piece that must be lined up (see photo). Because this one is small and difficult, I utilized smaller stitches.

Tie your thread off.

Sew the Second Body Piece to the Middle Piece in Step 7.

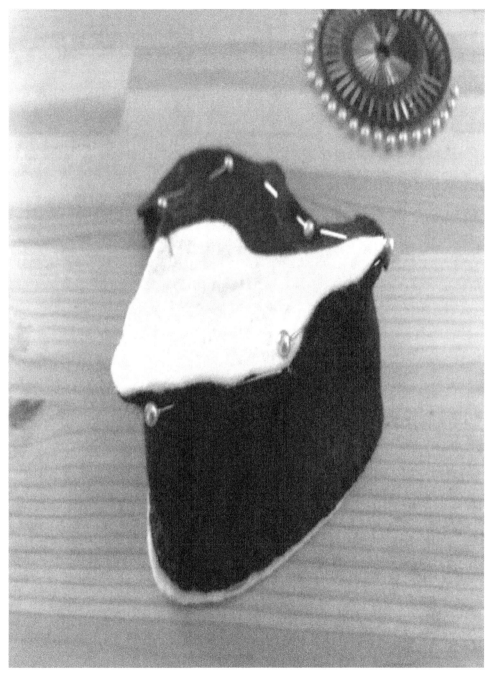

Connect the second body component to the opposite side of the middle piece.

You might wish to use pins to keep everything in place.

To attach the pieces, use a blanket stitch.

If you need a refresher on how to join it, go back to steps 4, 5, and 6.

Step 8: Fill Up Your Hoiho!

The top of your body pieces will still be open (where the hoiho's head will eventually be).

Fill the hoiho with your hobby fill through this hole.

You can also use cotton wool or the inner lining of an old cushion.

It's up to you how chonky your hoiho is (but keep in mind that hoiho can gain more than 40% of their usual body mass before moulting). Some reach a weight of exceeding 8.5 kg before losing its feathers).

Step 9: Sew the top of the body pieces together.

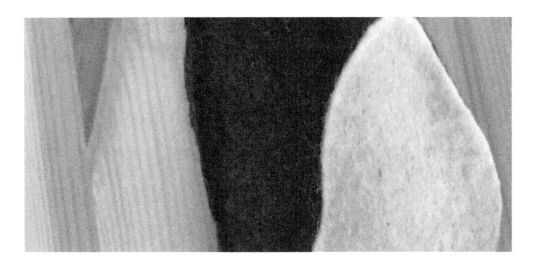

Sew the top of the body sections closed with a blanket stitch using a new piece of thread.

Glue the Headband Piece to the Body Pieces in Step 10.

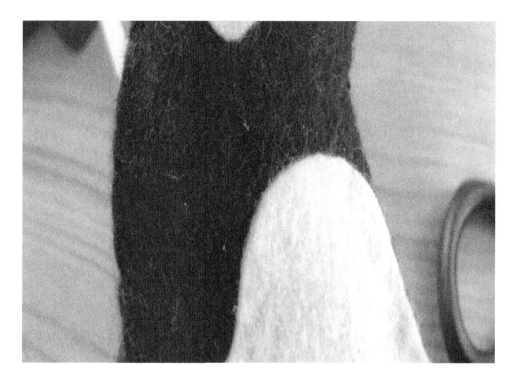

The headband is worn around the back of your hoiho's head.

Before you glue it, set it on the body pieces and secure it with a pin.

Once you're satisfied with the position, use your hot glue gun to adhere it to the body sections.

Step 11: Glue the Beak and Body Pieces Together

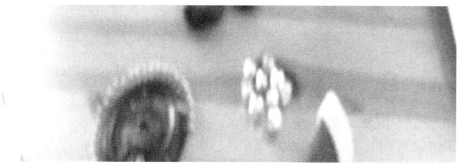

To begin, glue the beak parts together at the tip.

After that, distribute the beak pieces and place one on each side of the body parts.

Pin them in place first to check how they appear before you glue them. I observed that if I positioned the beak in a certain way, my hoiho appeared depressed (which is fair, since they are one of the rarest penguins in the world).

Once you're satisfied with the position, use your hot glue gun to adhere it to the body sections.

Step 12: Attach the Eyes

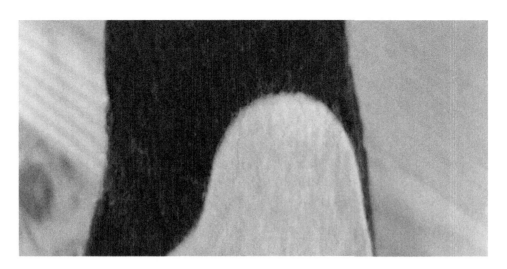

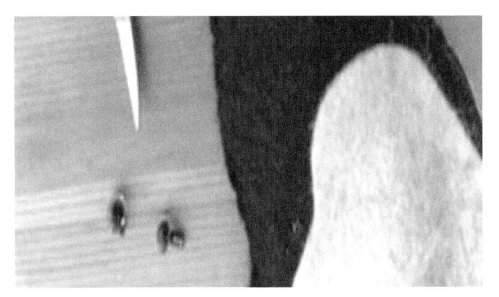

There are a few different types of eyeballs you can utilize.

The first step is to make a pair of eyeballs out of felt. These will have to be glued on.

The second method is to employ crystal eyeballs. These are typically used to make teddy bears and may be found at your local craft store. To wear them, carefully punch a hole through both the headband and the body piece. I did this with the point of some nail scissors. Take your time and be cautious! It's easy to enlarge the hole. Screw the eyeballs in once you've made a large enough hole. To keep them in place, I added a dab of hot glue.

Googly eyes could also be used.

Step 13: Create Hoiho's Santa Hat

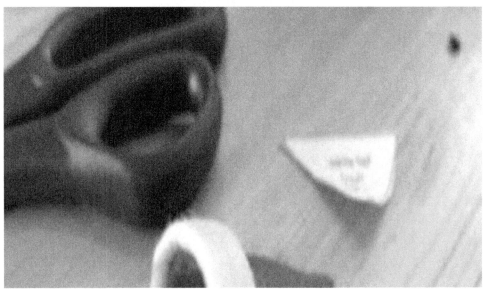

Using a blanket stitch, sew the edges of the Santa hat piece together. I only used one piece of thread, so it was beautiful and fine.

Glue the band piece around the hat's bottom edge.

Add a Hanger to Your Santa Hat in Step 14

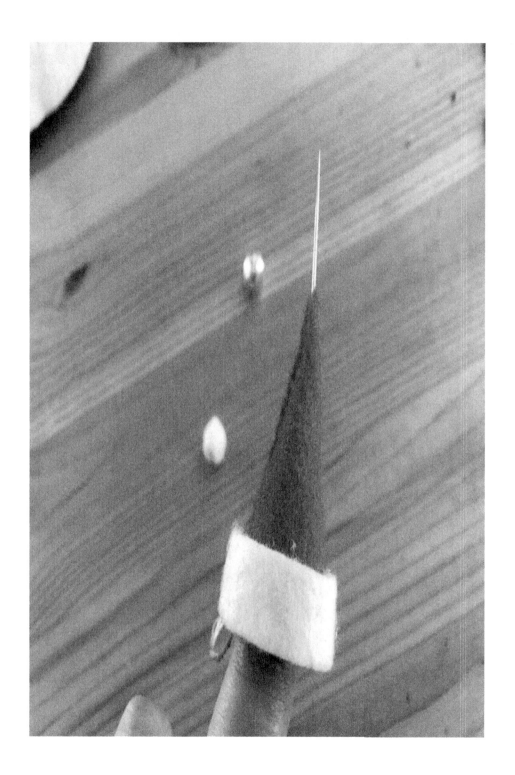

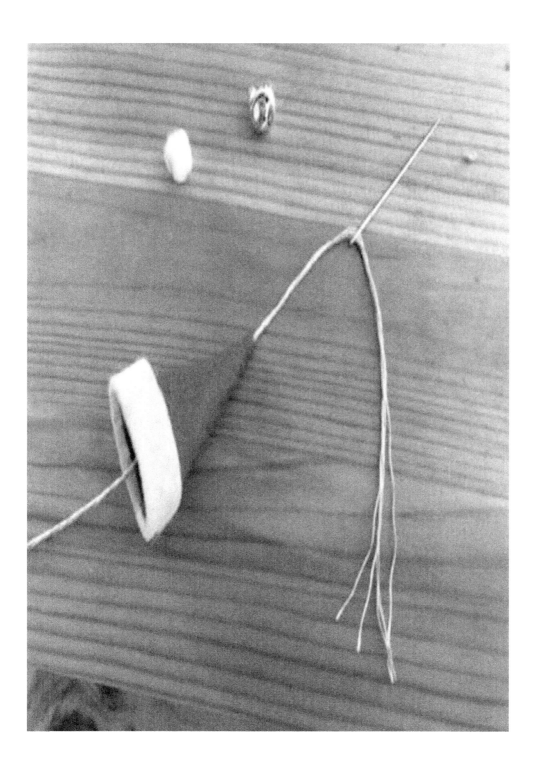

Now, add a hanger to your Santa hat using your silver or gold cotton so the hoiho can dangle from your Christmas tree.

There may be a more efficient way to complete this step, but here's how I did it...

Thread your needle through the top of the Santa hat. Don't go all the way through.

Thread your needle through your pom-pom. Don't go all the way through.

To make a loop, thread your needle and thread through your pom-pom. This is going to be your hanger.

Thread your needle back through the top of the santa hat. If you mistakenly pull the loop back through, you'll have to start over. Remove your needle from the thread.

Tie a knot at the bottom of the threads properly.

Pull your loop all the way through the top.

Step 15: Adhere the Santa Hat to Your Hoiho!

This is where you may can add extra Christmas jingle by inserting a bell into the hat.

Use pins to secure the hat to your hoiho's head before gluing it on. Ensure that the seam is in the back.

When you're satisfied with the placement, run a line of glue along the edge of each side of the Santa hat and stick it on. Remember that this is what will keep your hoiho on the tree, so make sure it's properly fastened.

Step 16: Good day, Hoiho!

Congrats you're done with this project; if you have been working
with me!

Consider crafting another unique project for yourself if you want to make hoiho exceptionally happy this Christmas.

CHAPTER FOUR

The Proposal Pillow (DIY)

So you want to get married, don't you?

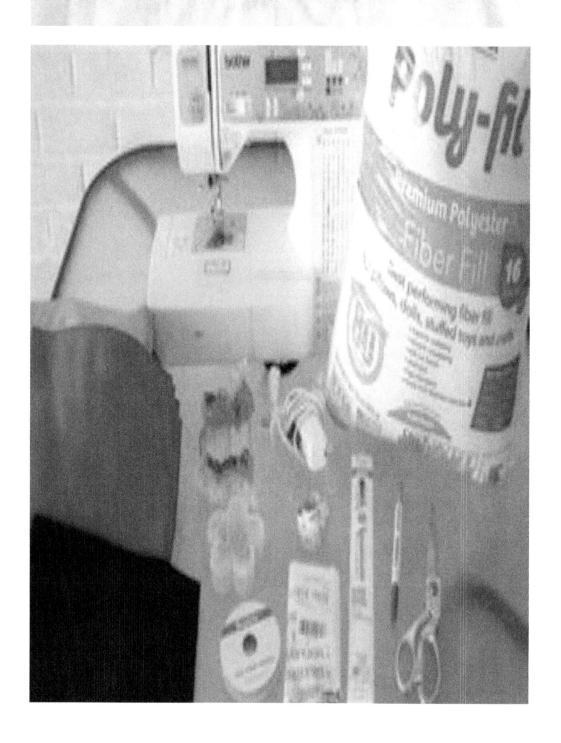

You want to give your special someone your heart (pun intended), but you're looking for an emotional and one-of-a-kind way to do so? The finest heartfelt gift, in my opinion, is one that you make yourself.

You could go with the standard dozen roses and a ring, but where's the heart in that? 445 roses, a ring, an emotional picture (or other memory) framed in a studded "diamond" ribbon, and a secret pocket to include a surprise for the love of your life (if you and the ring weren't enough)! Not to mention the practicality of a heart-shaped pillow that will last forever...not what's to love? This pillow will put your special someone to sleep...er, I mean, in love.

Supplies require in this project

- A sewing machine.

- Needle for ballpoint pen

- General-purpose machine needle

- 2 yards fabric (I used a polyester curtain from Goodwill)

- Coordinating thread

- Poly-filing (or any filling)

- A hot glue gun and a large supply of glue sticks

- 50 sheets of 9" × 12" x 2 mm red felt (23 cm x 30 cm x 2 mm)

- Pins

- 7" gold zipper on jeans/coat (on white backing)

- Marker for fabric

- Fabric shears

- Ribbon in gold and "diamond"

- One-eighth yard clear vinyl

- Poster board, card stock, thin cardboard, or thick paper scraps (must be at least 20" x 12")

- Trace around a circle with a circle object (3" in diameter)

- Cutter rotary

I was intending to use the black felt for something else, but I changed my mind. As a result, you won't require it.

First, iron the fabric.

1 Synthetic • Sintético • Sy…

2 Nylon • Silk • Seda • Soie

3 Polyester Rayon • Rayon • …

4 Blend • Mezcla • Meld

5 Wool • Lana • Laine

6 Cotton Linen • Algodón Lino • …

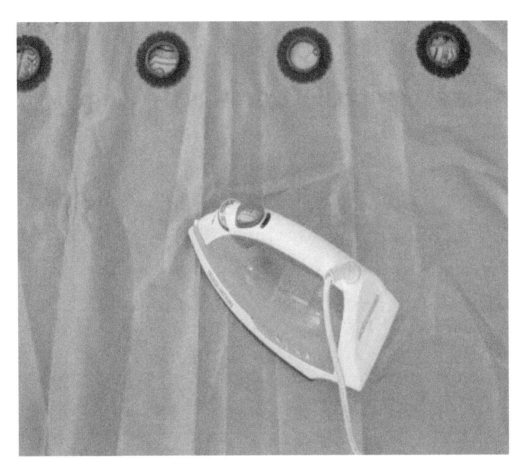

I'm thinking of using the grommets for another project in the future.

Because the cloth I was using was 100 percent polyester, I set the iron to setting #3.

I saw a lot of deep wrinkles that wouldn't come out after ironing. If you have the same issue, don't worry because the wrinkles won't show up in the finished cushion.

Step 2: Cut out a heart

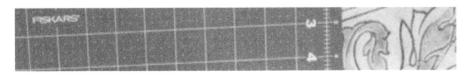

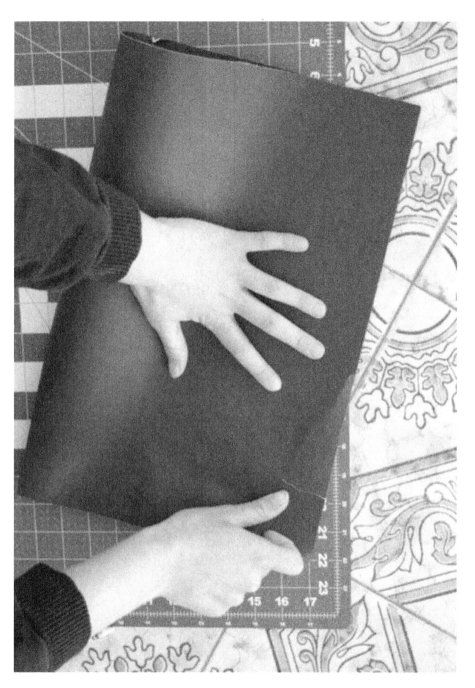

Fold your scrap poster board in half (so that it is even on both sides once cut).

Draw a heart that is about 10" broad from the center fold to the edge and 12" height.

Cut out the heart form, then unfold it to reveal the heart pattern.

Step 3: Cut a heart out of fabric

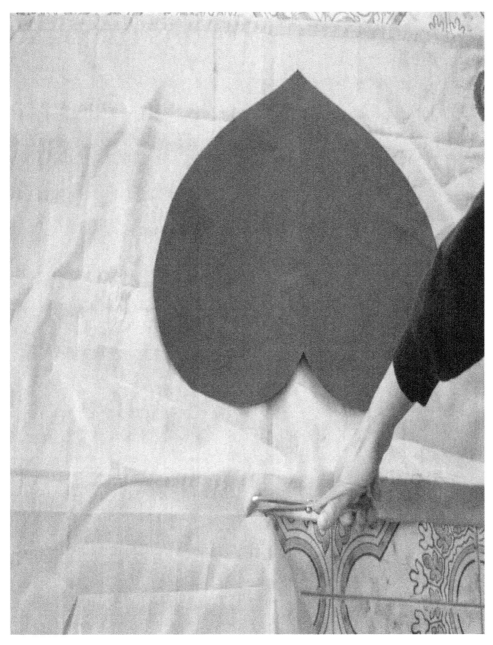

71

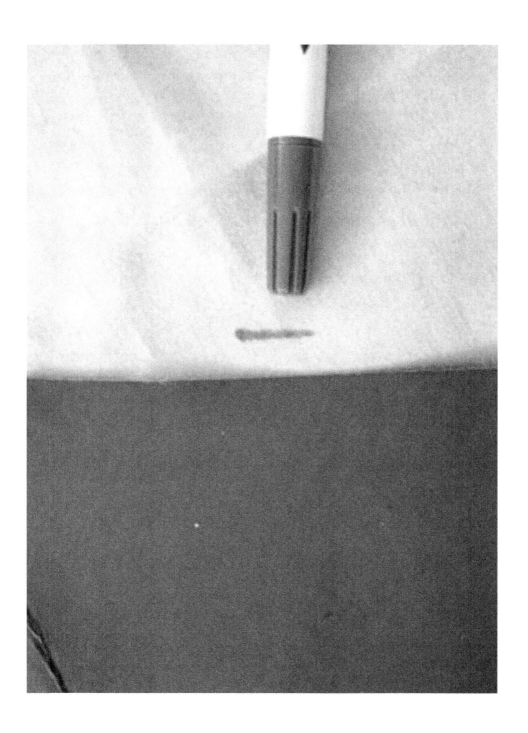

Make a heart pattern out of your fabric. If necessary, trim the fabric to a manageable size (leaving enough fabric so that it is more than double the length of the heart width, so 42" or more).

Cut the fabric in half (so it will make two pieces with one cut).

Ensure you Mark a 1/2" seam allowance around the heart with your fabric marker. Along this line, cut the fabric.

After that, trace the heart onto the fabric (so you can have a reference line for sewing).

Step 4: Zipper & Adjustments

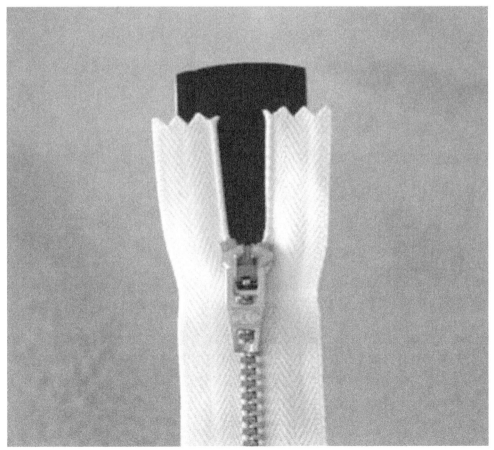

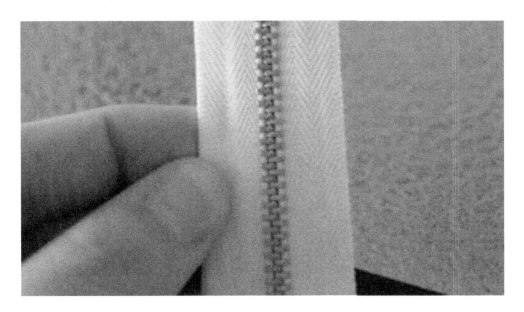

I used a gold 7" long jeans zipper with a white background.

You will use the following sewing machine settings throughout this Instructable:

• Stitching Straight

• Stitch length = 2.5

• Stitch width = 3.5

Now, these settings are specific to utilizing 100% polyester cloth, which is what I did.

However, before proceeding with this project, I strongly advise you to test stitch settings on a scrap piece of your own fabric.

Use a thread that is the same color as your fabric. As you can see, I had to use white thread since the matching thread kept bunching up in my machine's bobbin section for some unexplained reason. I'm not sure why.

You'll also need a zipper foot to install the zipper (however, you can do it without a zipper foot, if necessary).

Step 5: Label the Zipper

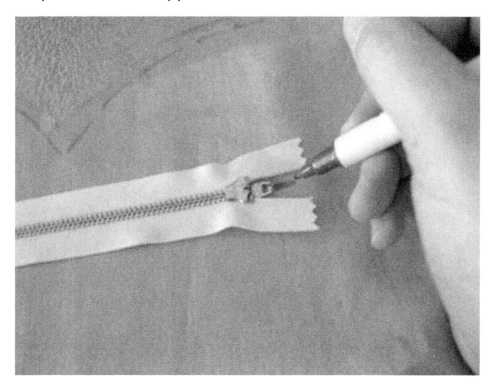

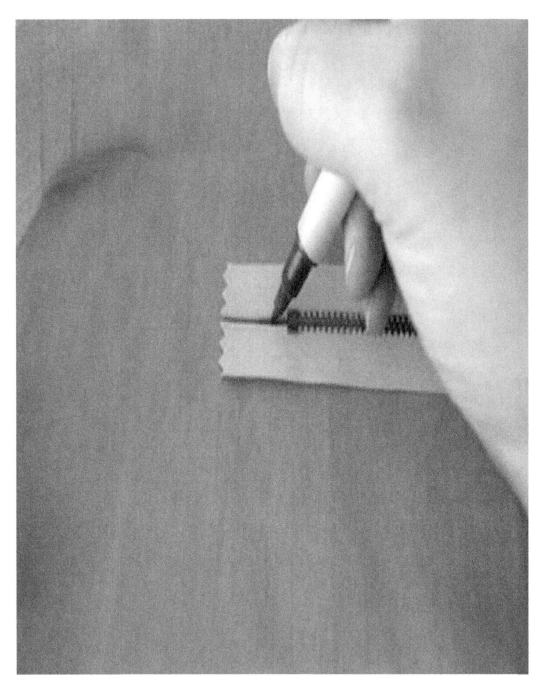

Place the zipper wrong-side-up on top of the wrong-side of the fabric on the heart piece that will be your back piece.

Mark the beginning and end of the zipper (the gold section, not the white backing).

Step 6: Make an opening.

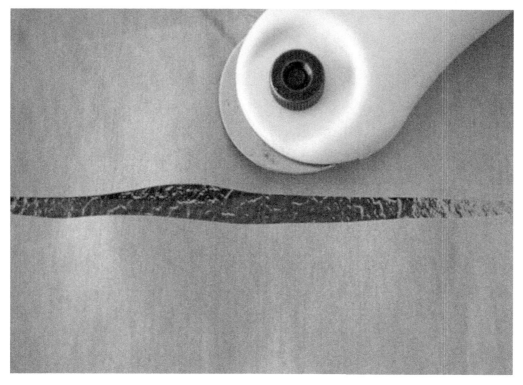

Cut a straight line between your markings with a ruler (or a straight edge).

I prefer to use a rotary cutter for this, but scissors will suffice if you don't have one.

If you cut it too long, there will be gaps on either end.

Step 7: Secure Zipper Side 1 with a safety pin.

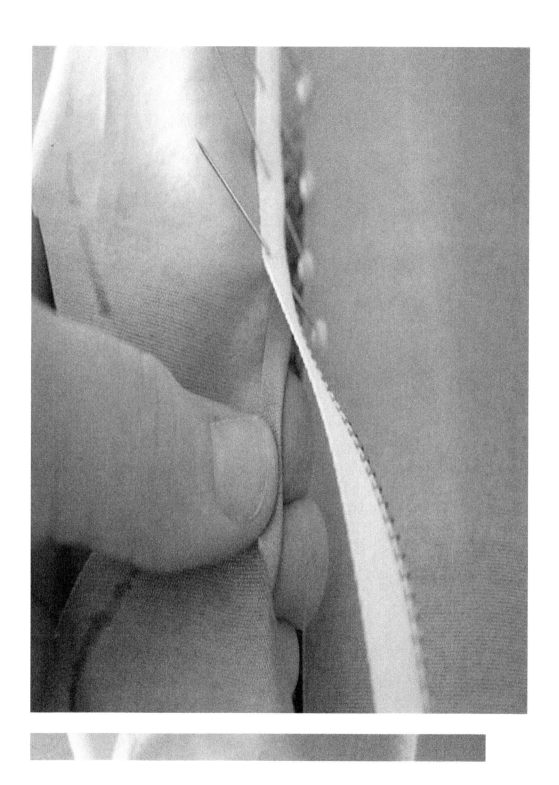

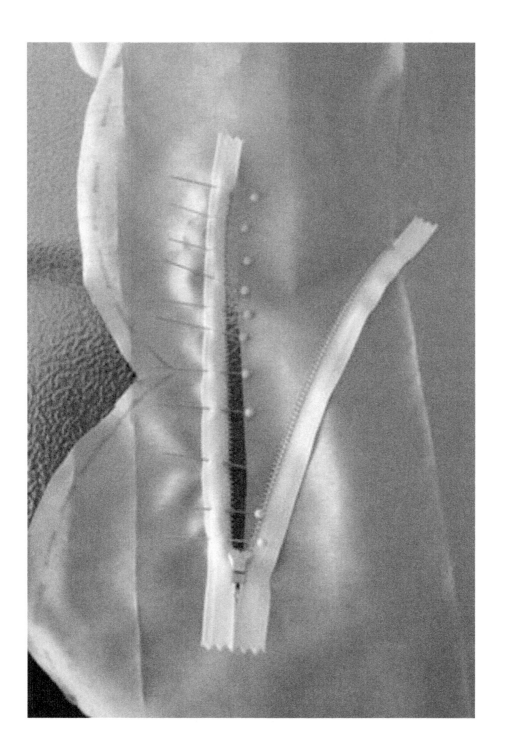

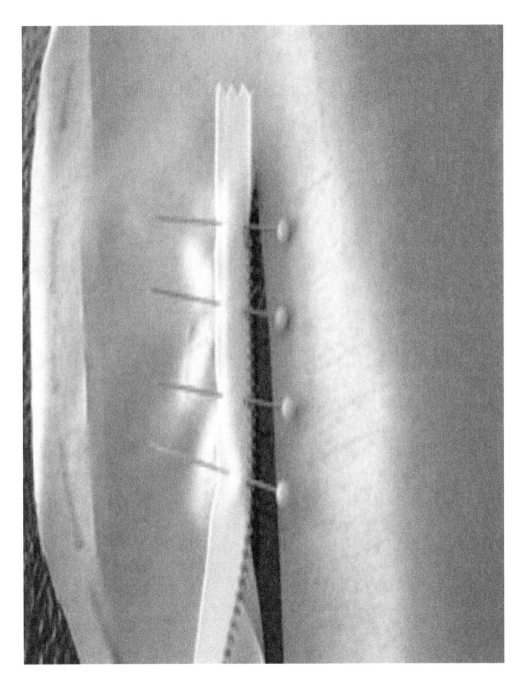

I won't lie: I'm not the best at putting zippers in.

I didn't use a basting stitch to attach the zipper. As I pinned, I just folded the fabric back (see pictures).

Please keep in mind that I unzipped the zipper to pin one side at a time.

Step 8: Sew Zipper Side 1 together.

Next, I sewed with my zipper foot as close to the zipper teeth as possible on the right side of the fabric.

Step 9: Repetition

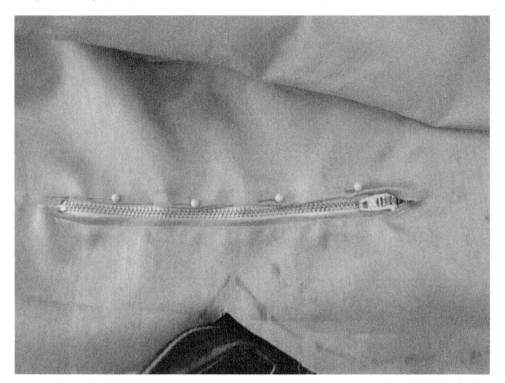

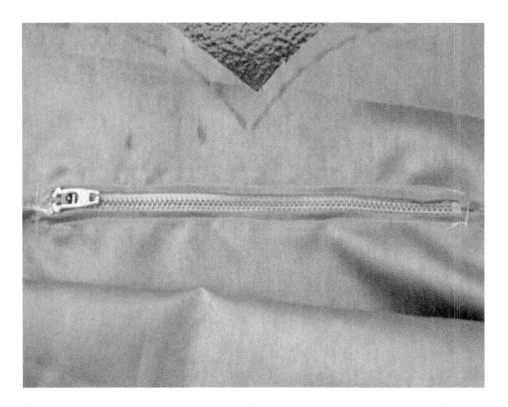

Then I repeated on the opposite side, sewing straight lines across both short sides of the zipper to finish it off.

Again, my thread was white, but if it fits your cloth, it shouldn't show much.

Step 10: Measure for the Pocket

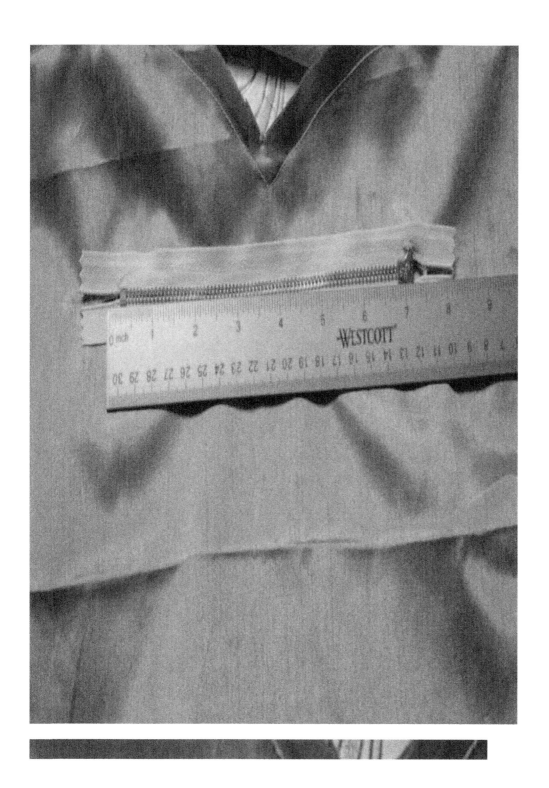

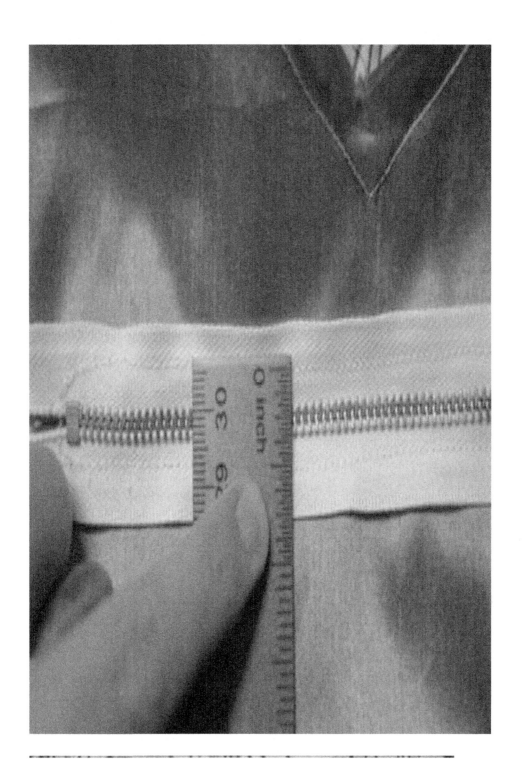

7½"

5" Piece 1 + ½" seam allowance (¼"ea.side)

7½"

4⅞" + ½" seam allowance
Piece 2 (¼"ea.side)

4x6 picture

To make the pocket on the interior of the back of the cushion, cut off two pieces of cloth.

First of all, you take the measurement of the distance from end to end, plus 1/2" on each side. This will ensure that the pocket covers the entire zipped area.

Then, measure the distance from the centre of the white backing's top to the middle of the white backing's bottom. The spacing between mine was 5/8" (see the second picture for clarity). This is the distance between the tops of the shorter and taller pieces.

Make a blueprint for your two parts using your measurements.

Mine were 7-1/2" x 5" and 7-1/2" x 4-3/8."

Furthermore, add a 1/2" seam allowance overall (to use 1/4" seams), and the final dimensions are 8" x 5-1/2" for the taller piece and 8" x 4-7/8" for the shorter piece.

Step 11: Measure, Cut, and Pin

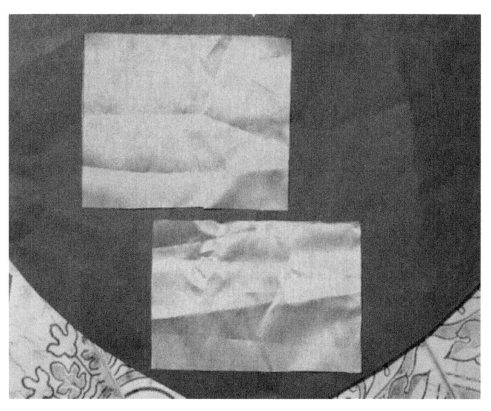

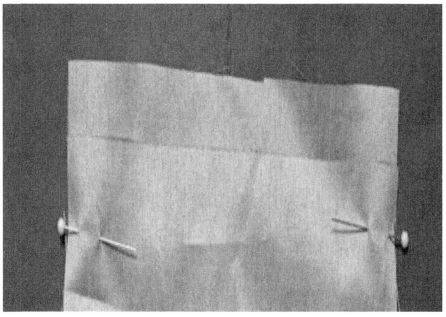

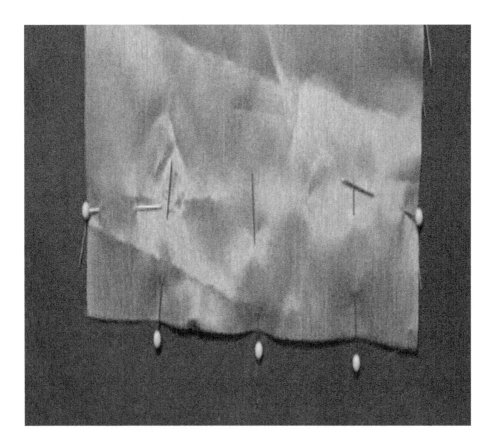

Measure those proportions onto the cloth, cut it, and pin it right sides together.

Step 12: Replace the Machine Needle

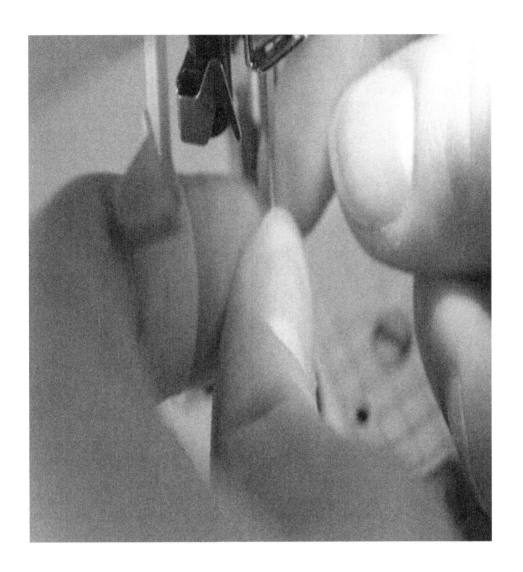

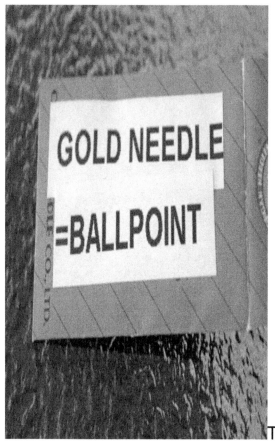This step is required if you are using 100 percent polyester fabric, silk, satin, or knitted fabric.

If you're using a sturdier fabric, such as cotton, wool, or even denim, you can omit this step.

When stitching fabric to fabric, you will need to switch from an all-purpose sewing machine needle to a ballpoint needle.

Because the needle has a gentler point, this prevents small tears in the cloth during stitching.

When sewing fabric on other materials, return your machine's needle to the all-purpose needle.

Otherwise, the harder substance may break your ballpoint needle.

Step 13: Sew Pocket

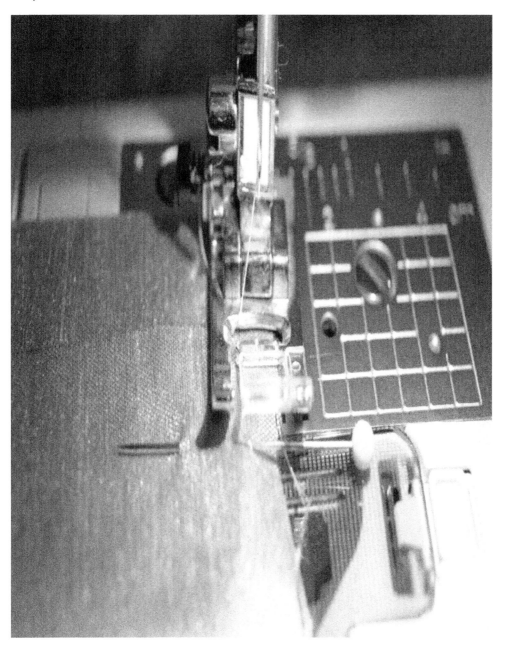

Sew around the three sides of the pocket, leaving the top open.

Step 14: Trim the Corners

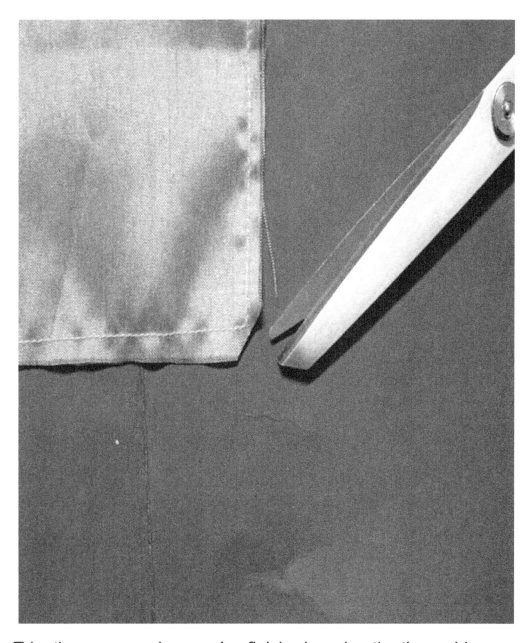

Trim the corners when you've finished sewing the three sides.

This gives you finer corners when you turn the pocket right-side-out.

Step 15: Turn the pocket right side out.

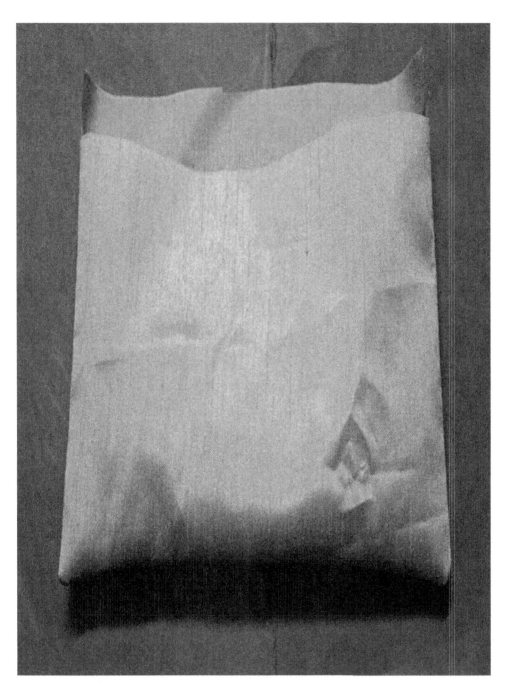

Turn the pocket right-side out.

Change your machine needle back to all-purpose.

Step 16: Sew the Short Side to the Zipper

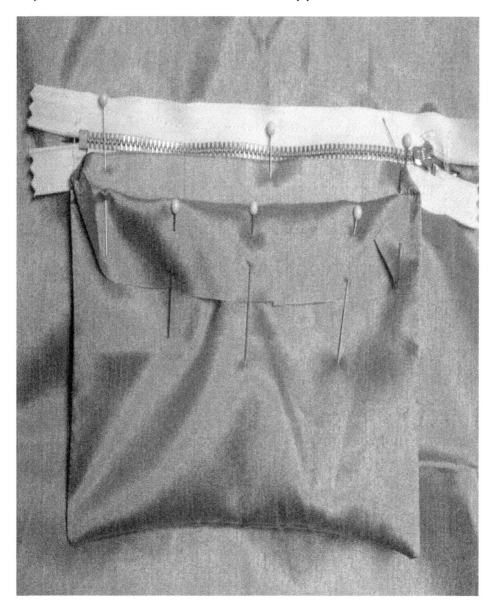

Pin only the short side of the zipper to the bottom white backing piece.

I used pins to keep the longer piece in place so I didn't sew over it.

Sew the shorter piece to the zipper backing.

Step 17: Sew the Long Side to the Zipper

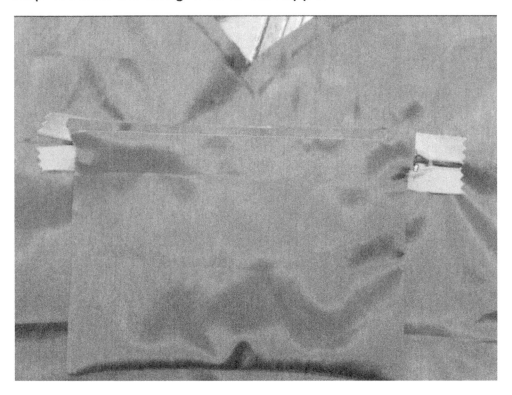

When finished, unpin the longer piece and pin it to the zipper's top white backing piece.

Sew the fabric to the zipper component.

Step 18: Create an Outer Picture Pocket

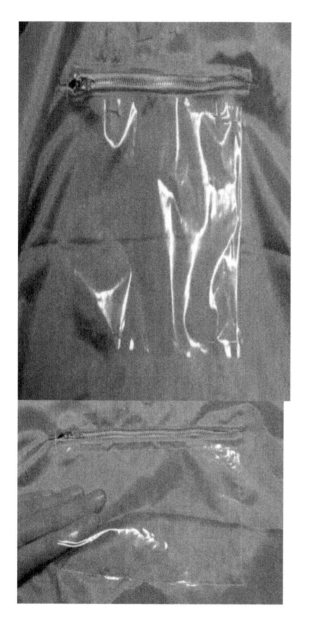

To build the outside transparent pocket for holding a picture or a card, first measure the clear vinyl.

I wanted to be able to fit a 4 x 6 photo (or smaller) in it, so I sized my vinyl to be 4-1/2" x 6-1/2."

Pin the vinyl to just under the zipper on the right side of the fabric.

MAKE SURE your pocket underneath is pinned up so you don't pin or sew the vinyl to the inner pocket.

Sew the pocket on all three sides except the left (so on the top, right side, and bottom).

Step 19: Add a Decorative Frame

Place your decorative ribbon between the top of the clear pocket and the zipper (it should cover the bottom zipper stitches and the top of the vinyl stitching). I positioned the ribbon so that it was as long as the clear pocket, plus one extra square on each side.

Glue the ribbon down. Glue each square independently.

Continue around the pocket, aligning up the squares as best you can, until it resembles a frame.

NOTE: When adding the decorative ribbon to the left side (where the vinyl opens), leave about 1/2" of room between the opening and the ribbon. This way, you can still easily insert pictures/cards into the vinyl pocket.

Step 20: Sew the Pillow Case

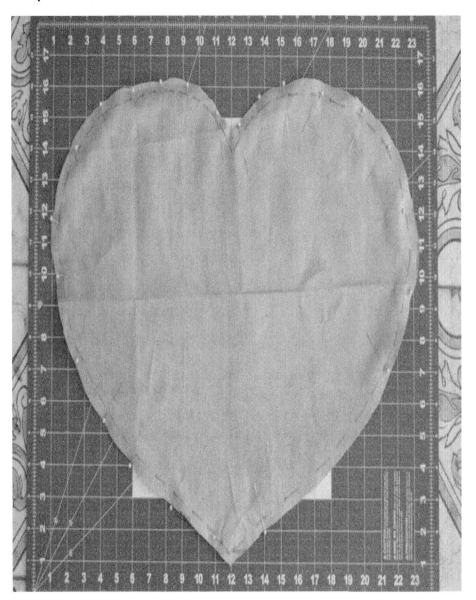

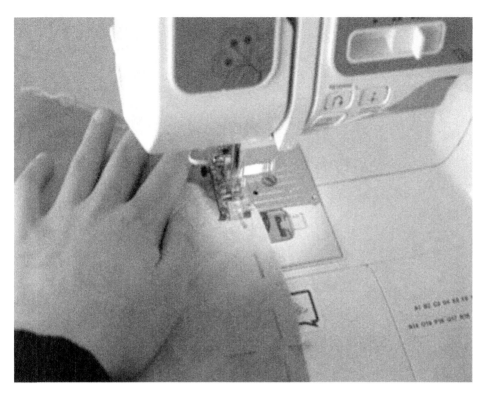

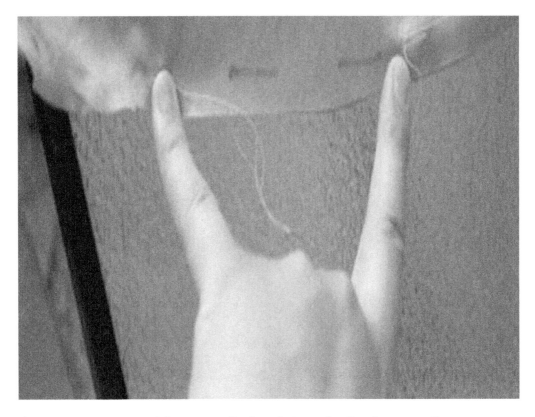

Change your machine needle back to a ballpoint needle.

Pin the two heart-shaped pieces right sides together.

Sew around the heart along the line you drew when you traced the black poster board onto the heart. This leaves about a 1/2" seam.

Make sure to leave a gap to turn your pillow case right side out.

Step 21: Turn Right-Side Out

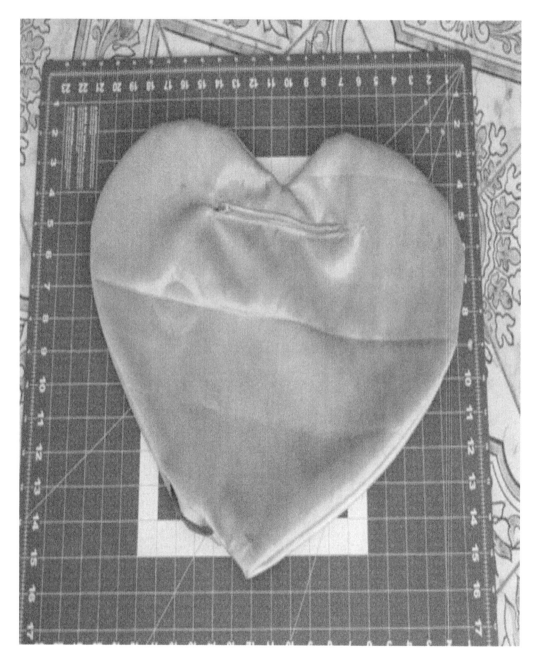

Simply place your hand within the gap you left open and begin flipping it right-side out.

Step 22: Cut Poster Board

Reduce the original poster board to the size of the sewed heart.

Step 23: Roll it up

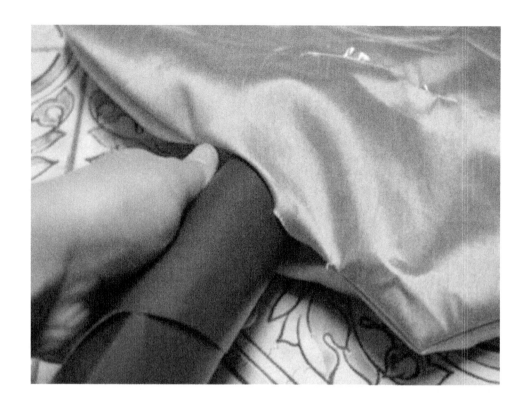

Roll up the poster board, slide it into the pillow case, and smooth it down to the desired form.

This will keep the cloth from gluing shut when you add the roses.

It will also help the finished cushion retain a wonderful heart shape.

NOTE: It adds no stiffness to the final pillow (you won't even notice it's there in the end).

Step 24: Make Rose Circles

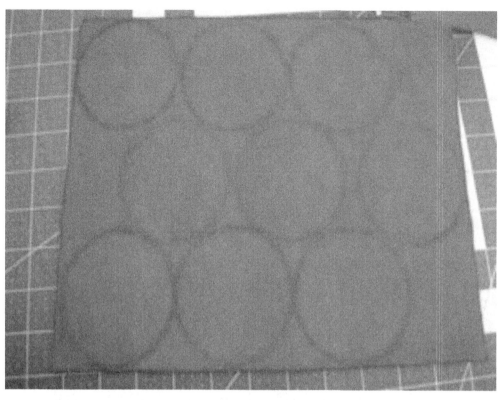

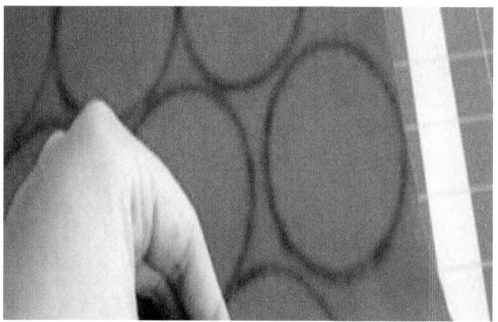

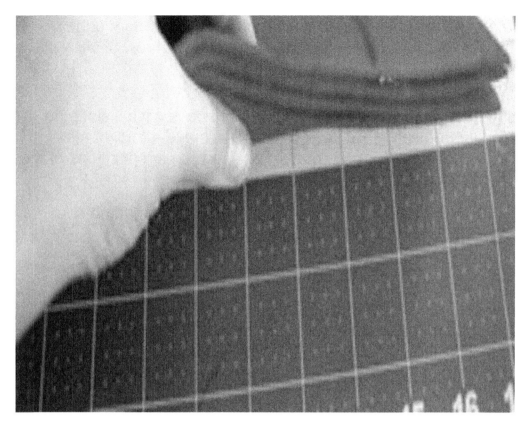

Place your 3" circle object on the felt. Using a fabric marker, trace around it.

(I had to use a washable marker because my fabric marker ran out, but I would definitely recommend using a vanishing ink fabric marker.)

First, trace three longitudinal circles from left to right, with the first circle on the farthest left nearly touching the edge of the felt (see picture 3 for clarity).

Next, trace ONE circle on the far right, nearly brushing the edge of the felt.

Then, trace the THIRD ROW of circles along the bottom edge of the felt from right to left, aligning them up with the first row of circles.

Finally, fill in the middle two circles.

Putting more than one circle in a row at a time is critical since not all felt pieces are exactly the same size. To achieve a total of nine circles from each piece, you may have to switch the positions of the final two circles in the center row.

Stack 5-6 more pieces of felt on top of the finished marked sheet of felt. Keep an eye on their measurements.

Place a pin through the center of each circle before cutting to keep the pieces together. This method makes it a breeze to cut out 445 flowers in a matter of minutes! I think it's an excellent choice!) Circles should be cut off. Repeat this process until all sheets are cut.

How to Make a Rose is the 25th step.

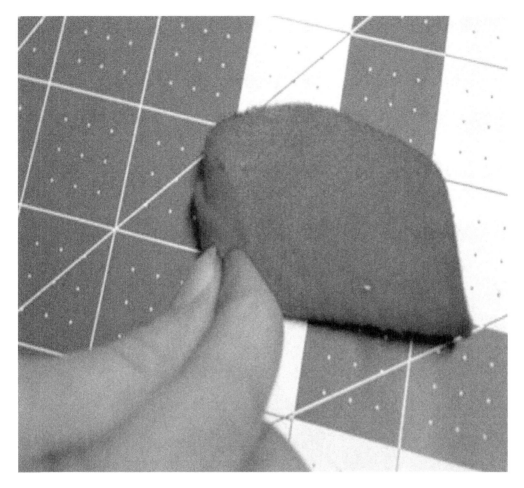

Here Are Five More Illustrations

Remove all of the felt stacks from their pins.

Follow these steps to create a rose:

When you fold a circle in half, leave about 1/4" space between the two points (see second picture).

Make a complete turn of the folded circle.

Make a rose effect by rolling tightly away from your body, but leave a small piece of felt unrolled at the bottom (fourth picture).

To secure the unrolled felt to the rolled rose, apply a small dab of glue to the area.

• Roll the rose over the glue again and again to secure it.

• Allow the adhesive to dry for about 5 seconds before removing the clamp.

Voila! We still need 444 more of these! For the front of your pillow, or as many as necessary.

In this step 26, you should begin at the center.

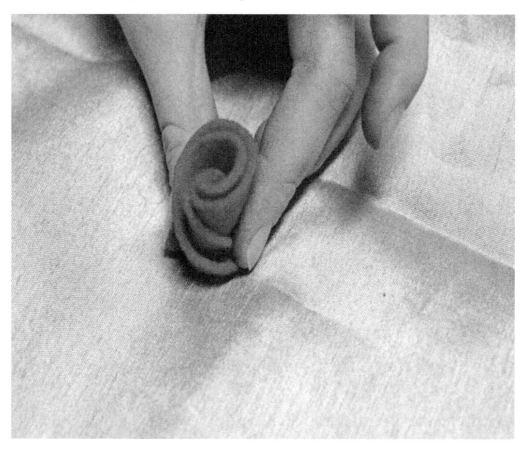

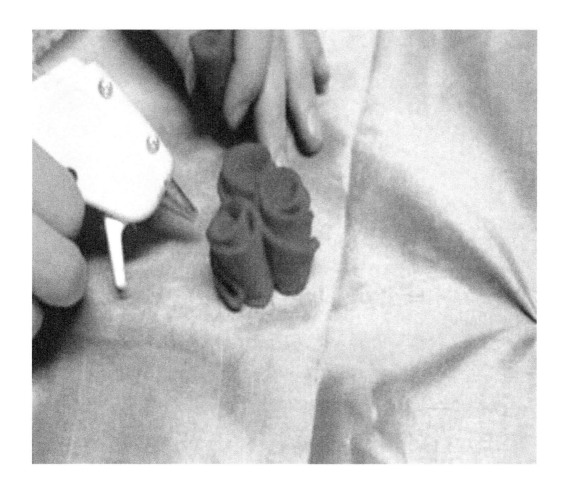

In the middle of the pillow, place a felt rose (start in the center and work your way out).

In order to have three roses, glue another one immediately next to the first one (see second picture).

Pull the flowers apart slightly to apply a dab of glue to each one, then reassemble them (or add glue to the backs of the new roses as your adding them). As long as you don't pack the roses too tightly, they will stay together.

The orientation of the roses and the size of the roses should be changed. Adding a bunch of roses to the sculpture adds visual interest and texture.

Continue Adding Roses in Step 27.

131

Once you've filled the pillow with roses, leave a small gap at the bottom so that you don't glue the gap shut (see picture two).

It's time to stow away

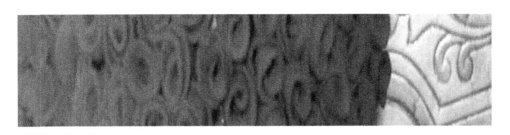

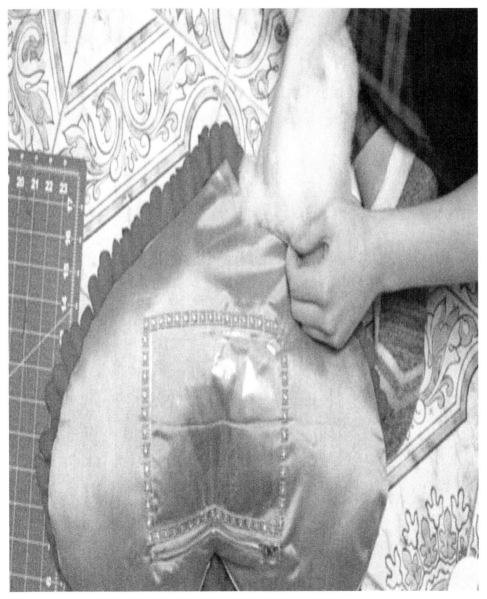

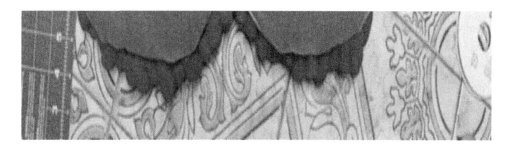

After filling the pillow with Poly-fil, start at one hump and work your way down to the open space.

Inspect for any lumps or bubbles that could be construed as "air" (places of no Poly-fil).

This is the last step.

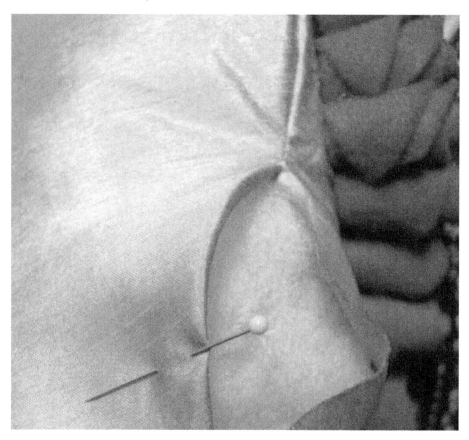

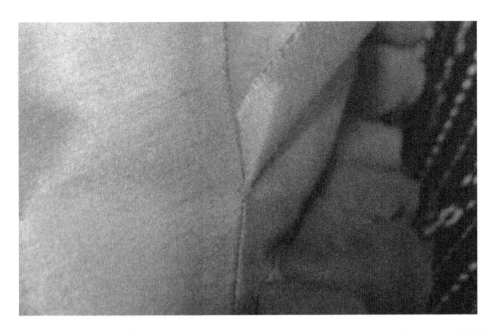

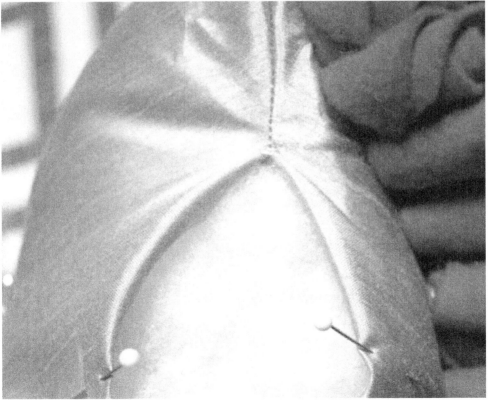

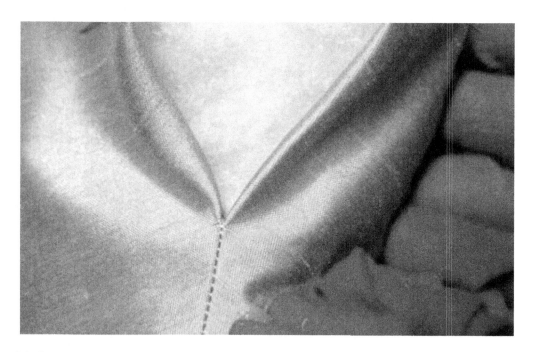

Make a hem by pinning both sides of the gap.

Blind Stitching is the final step in this guide

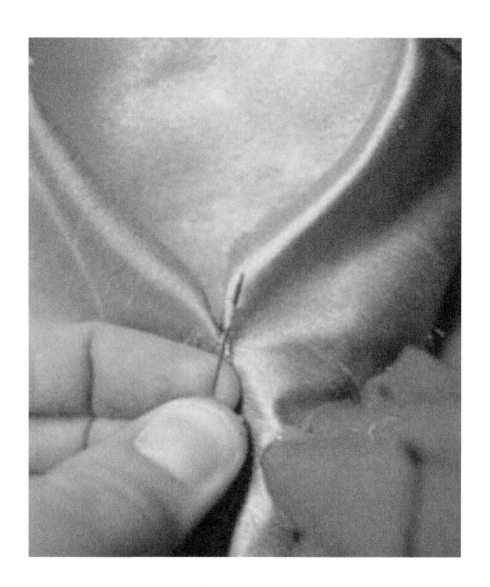

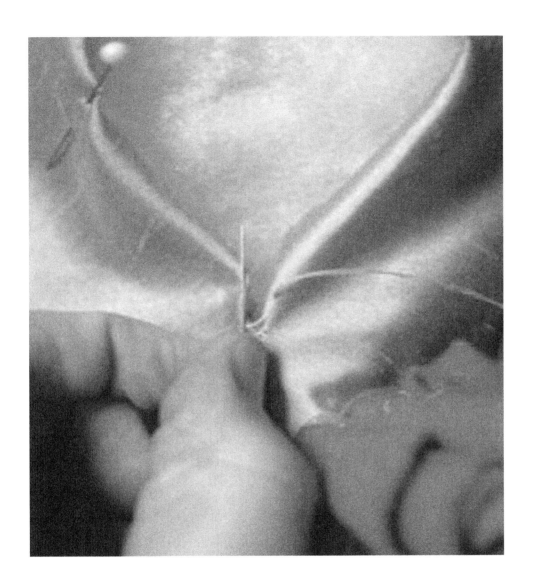

The closure should be sewn shut with a blind stitch.

To make a blind hem:

The needle should be threaded.

Pull the needle from the right side of the fabric hem to the underside of the fabric hem (use the first picture for clarity). Stitching will be concealed by this method.

Using a sewing needle, sew over the gap and into the hem of the opposite side (use the second picture for clarity).

Go through this side's hem by retracing your needle's path back to the stitch you just made, and then back over the gap (use the third picture for clarity).

The rungs of a ladder begin to form as the thread continues to pass over the gap (back and forth) and into the middles of the hem cloth (see the sixth picture).

Make an inconspicuous seam by squeezing the thread tight.

Pull the thread taut every few stitches until the entire seam has been completed.

It's time to wrap things up.

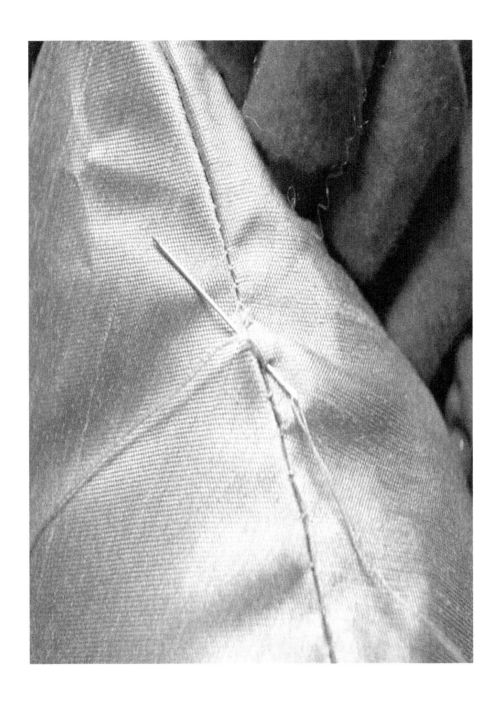

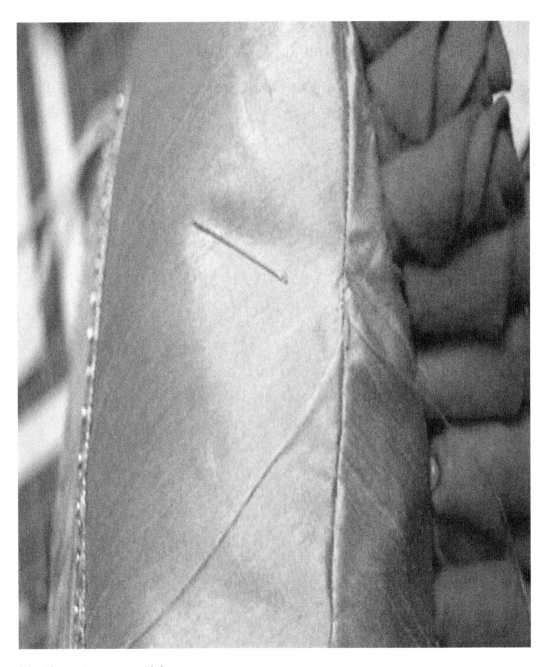

It's time to wrap things up:

1. Make a knot by coming up through the fabric's underside.

2. Make knots in the same place a few more times before moving on to the next location (like you did the first time).

3. Pull the needle out of a random portion of the cloth and insert it into the body of the pillow (through the seam where your knot is).

Using scissors, cut the thread.

Step 32: It's time to finish putting in the final roses!

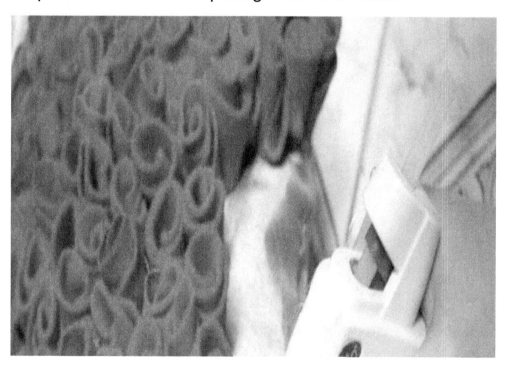

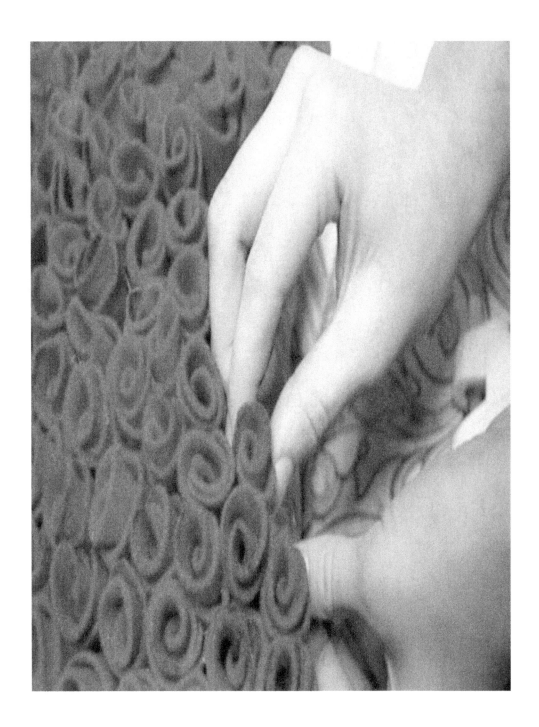

Once the pillow is filled and the gap is sewed, add the flowers to the empty space above the gap.

Step 33: Fill in the Gaps and Clean Up

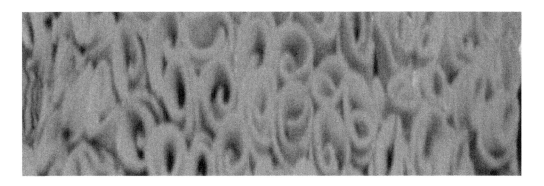

Filling the pillow will leave some gaps between the roses that need to be tended to. A dab of adhesive is all that is needed to fill in the space and then insert the rose.

As a result, there will also be small amounts of hot glue sludge. Find them, and get them out of the way.. Additionally, you can use a lint roller to get it looking its best.

Add a Photo or a Greeting Card in Step 34.

The clear vinyl pocket can be filled with a photograph or a card.

Finally, the 35th step has been completed!

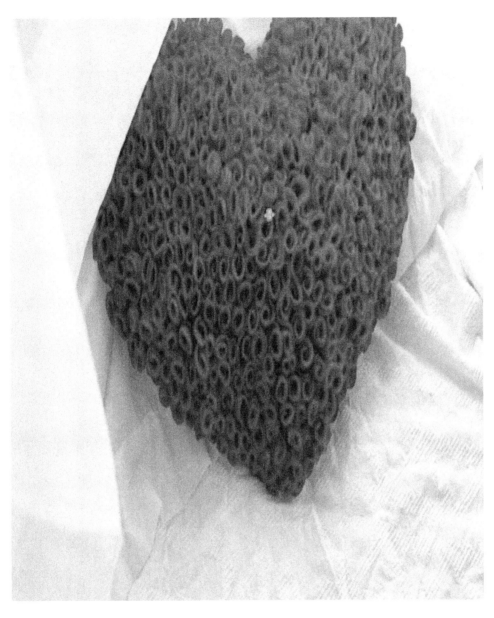

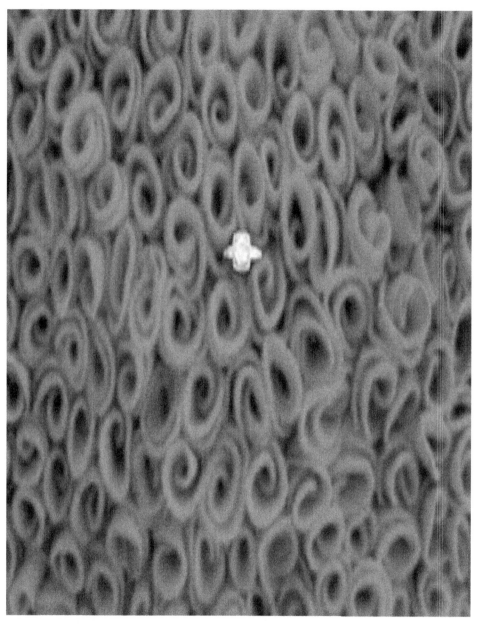

Voila! You've just finished the perfect proposal cushion for your
significant other!

If she accepts your proposal, you'll be all set!

When presenting the ring, you can either put it in the roses or put it in the pocket.

CHAPTER FIVE

Realistic Animal Needle Felting Techniques

You can shape, re-form, and create life-like animals with extraordinary attention to detail using the time-consuming process of needle felting, in which you repeatedly stab at loose wool fibers with a barbed needle.

This guide will teach you how to make a realistic ermine (also known as a cat snake!) using a wire armature using a variety of techniques.

Over the span of a month, I worked on this ermine for roughly 16 hours. While you can experiment as a beginner needle Felter, I recommend that you have some prior experience because these techniques gloss over how to shape your animal. Before getting into this book, I recommend that you try a few of faster, simpler needle felting crafts.

Best wishes!

Step 1: Gather Your Materials

This project will necessitate the following materials:

• felting needles in the following sizes: 36 (optional), 38, 40, and 42 (and higher if desired)

• roving of coarse wool (any color, but white is most common)

• Merino wool in white, black, brown, pink, and red (will vary depending on what you want to make)

• For whiskers, use genuine horse/alpaca hair or transparent fishing line.

•Wire loops on glass eyes

 A pipe cleaner

• razor-sharp scissors

• googly eyes

• thread and needle

• 15-plus hours

Step 2: Construct a Wire Armature

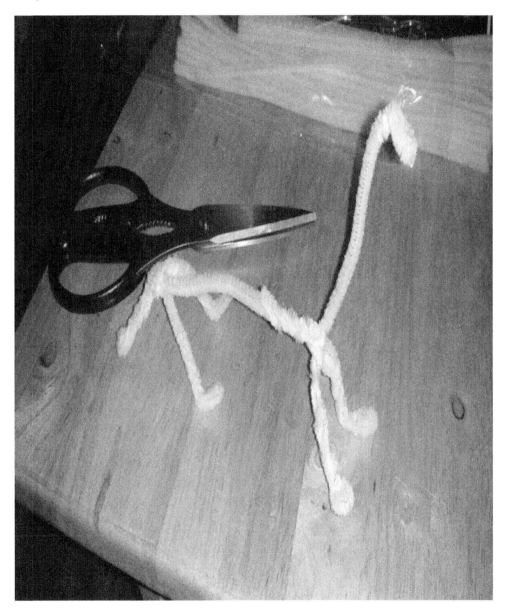

Once you've chosen your animal, create a wire armature out of pipe cleaners in the general shape of your animal. Fold in any wires since they will stab through your wool and are very sharp.

Step three:

Step 4: Wrap your head and body in roving wool.

For the body, start with rough "roving wool" with a coarse felting needle (36 or 38) and felt until you get a rough shape that holds together on its own (as pictured). Do not do the entire leg, simply the top "muscle," as it may become too fat after the layers of soft merino wool are applied.

After you've finished this, go to a higher felting needle (40), which will allow you to gradually felt a denser body. Begin designing your animal by layering and generating denser parts as needed. If you use a 42 or higher felting needle, your creation will become overly dense.

Step 5: Add Your Merino Wool Layer

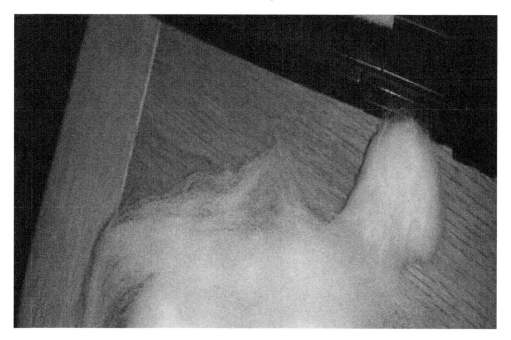

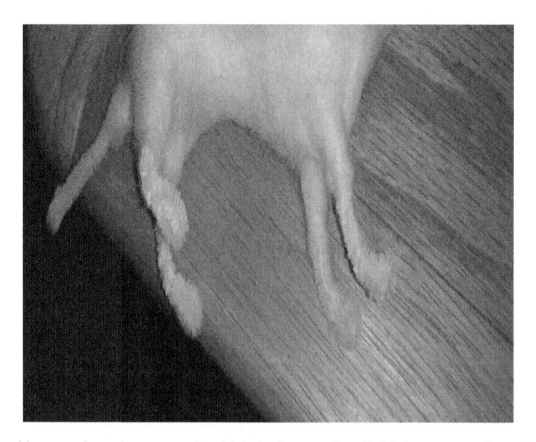

Use merino sheep wool, which is fine and soft. Using a very fine 42 felting needle, apply thin layers of wool to the body of your animal. To avoid a "striped" appearance, make sure the wool is aligned with the posture of your animal. Felt it evenly, making sure to cover all regions of the rough roving. This will necessitate numerous layers.

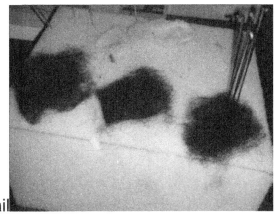

Step 6: Design the Tail

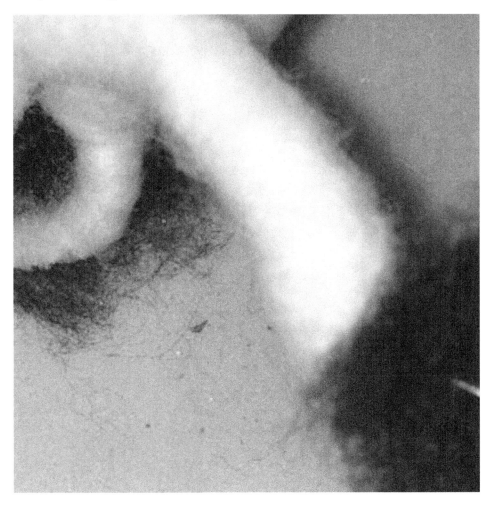

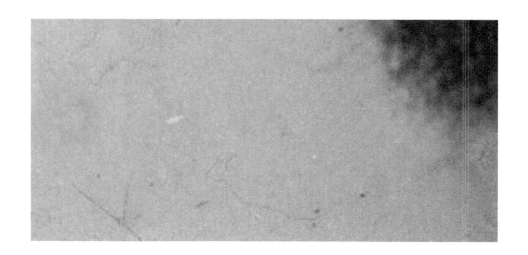

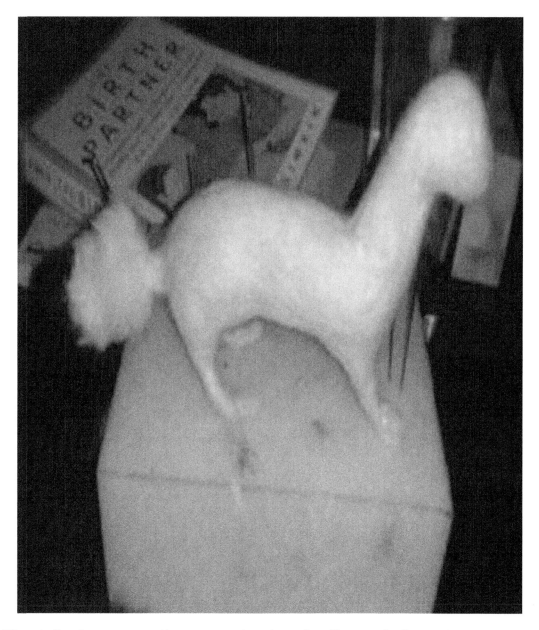

The tail takes some time to make, but the "loose fur" aesthetic is definitely worth the effort.

Begin by creating merino wool strips and dividing them into parts.

Fold each part in half and feel it onto the coarse roving in the center with a 42 needle. Felted to the sides in a variety of ways until the fur could handle a gentle tug;

Continue this process from the bottom up, making sure each area is near to the previous one to avoid spots.

Continue! Finally, cut the hairs so that they are all about the same length.

Step 7: Attach Ears

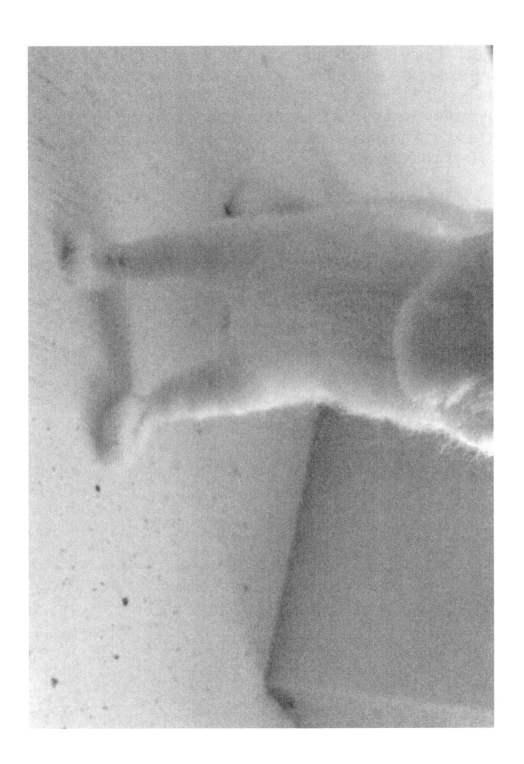

To make ears Make a rough form out of flat felt cloth and fray the ends using scissors. Wrap them in the roving of your choice, leaving the fray exposed. Using a 42 needle, felt the roving on the ear and felt the ears onto the head of the animal around the fray. Blend it onto the head and shape it suitably with merino roving, making sure the wool flows onto the neck.

Step 8: Shape the Head and Add Eyes

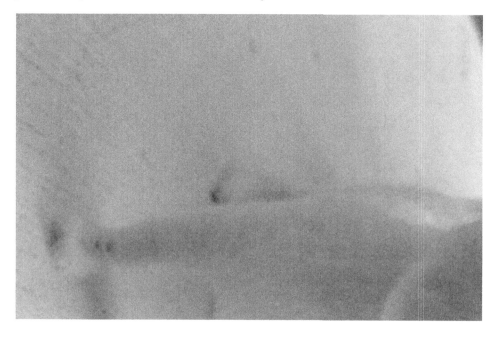

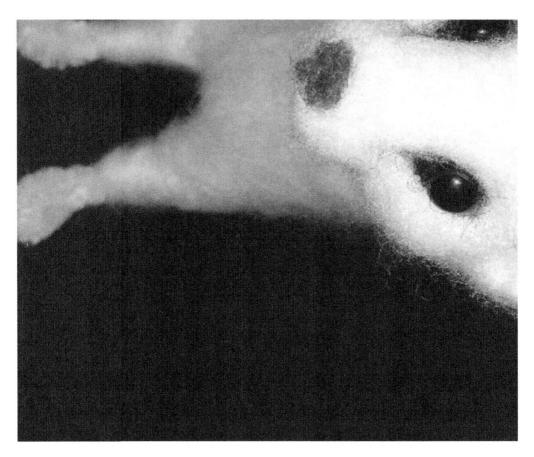

Shape the head and snout roughly by felting denser parts and adding/removing merino wool. Make sure the area around the eyes isn't too dense, as the eyes need to fit tightly.

Make use of glass eyeballs with wire loops. Using scissors or an exacto knife, cut indents and a slit into the wool. Thread the loop and pull the needle and thread through to the back of your animal's head. Pull it taut so that the wire enters the slit you made previously and knot the thread at the back.

Once both eyes are in place, cover the thread knots at the back of the head with merino roving. With the eyes in place, you can begin to accurately sculpt your animal's head and snout. Make extensive use of Google pictures!

Step 9: Include Paws

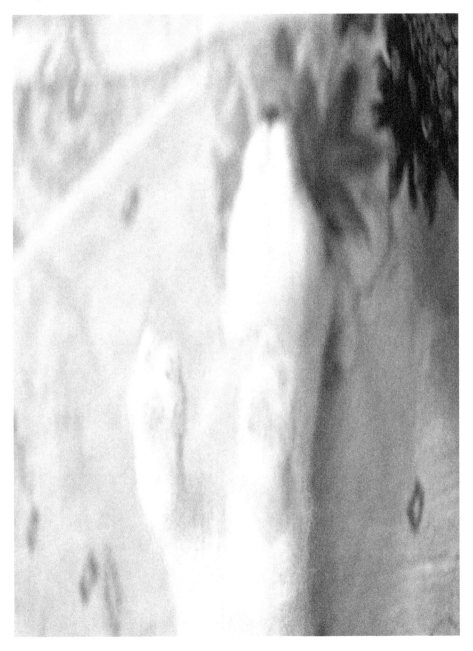

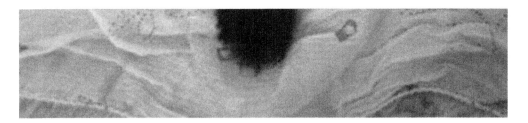

Wrap the bottom of the pipe cleaner in merino roving and felt until it's slightly dense. Make numerous loops and pull to generate the correct amount of indents for toes using a comparable color thread. Once finished, feel a small bit of merino between the toes to hide the thread.

Step 10: Include Specifics

This is my favorite section!

Again, using a 42 felting needle and a plethora of Google photos, add your details in appropriate colors. To improve the contour of the eyes, add darkness around them, feel a nose, and draw a mouth with straight lines of roving. Color inside the ears and on the paw pads. Fill in any details your animal may have, such as stripes or patches.

Make whiskers out of natural hair, such as horse or alpaca, or fishing line. Thread them through a needle and thread them through the snout, then secure them with super glue. To iron out any kinks in natural hair, use a hair straightener carefully in smoothing it.

Finishing Touches (Step 11)

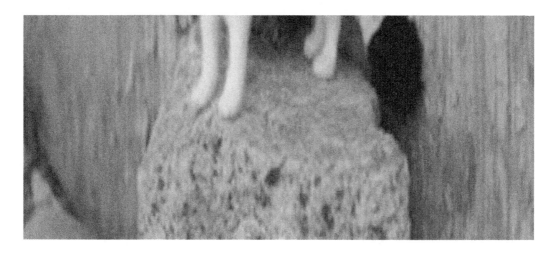

Give it one last look and felt any stray fibers with a 42 needle horizontally to give it a smoother appearance.

Using a sharp pair of scissors, carefully snip loose fibers.

Beautiful! A project like this one might take up to 15-20 hours to complete. Relax and enjoy the felting journey!

CHAPTER SIX

FELTED STRIPE CHRISTMAS STOCKINGS (DIY)

I spent the majority of the holiday season attempting to figure out how to build my ideal stockings. Stockings in red and white stripes made of felted wool. Ones that we hoped to have for the rest of our lives. I finally worked it out after MANY failed efforts and causing my entire house to smell like a barn (hint: wet felting is NOT my thing! lol!), and I couldn't be happier with how they turned out. Thank you to everyone who has followed and supported me along my lengthy journey to this point. LOL! Anyway, if you want to make your own, I have a lesson for you today!! I don't have a lot of step images because I wasn't sure if they were going to function when I made them, but I did my best to illustrate a tutorial for you anyhow. Let's get started!!

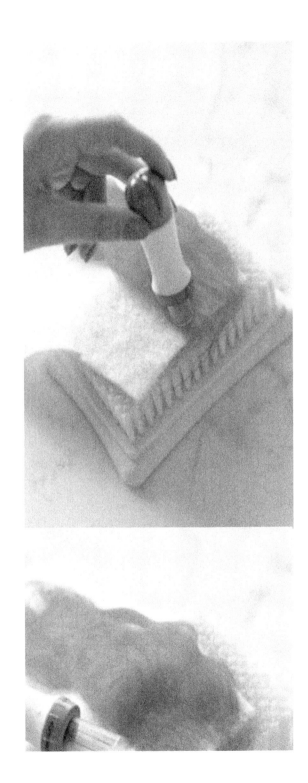

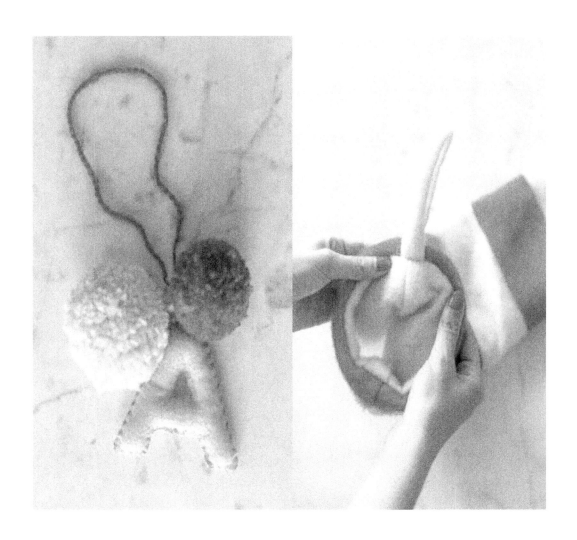

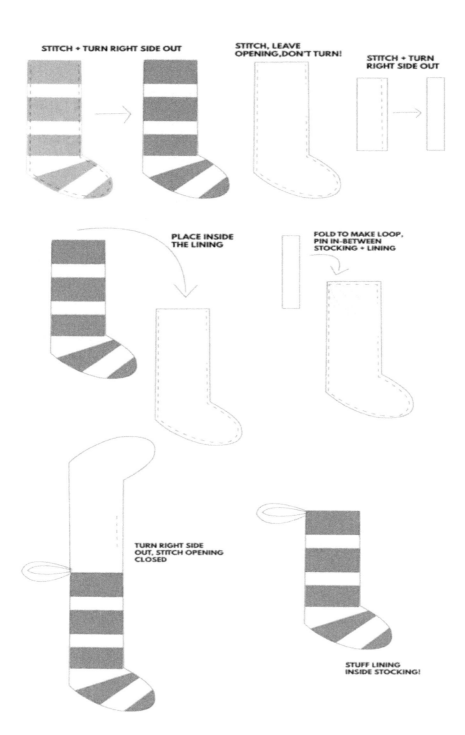

STITCH + TURN RIGHT SIDE OUT

STITCH, LEAVE OPENING, DON'T TURN!

STITCH + TURN RIGHT SIDE OUT

PLACE INSIDE THE LINING

FOLD TO MAKE LOOP, PIN IN-BETWEEN STOCKING + LINING

TURN RIGHT SIDE OUT, STITCH OPENING CLOSED

STUFF LINING INSIDE STOCKING!

FELTED STRIPE CHRISTMAS STOCKINGS (DIY)

Total time required: 3+ hours per stocking; though it depends on the individual.

Supplies require:

A large piece of paper (or a paper grocery bag) to serve as a template

Wool Felt in White/Cream (About 2 yards, if you are lining the stocking with felt too)

Roving in Red Wool

Mat for Needle Felting

Needle Felting Instrument

Machine for Sewing

Pins

Scissors

Making use of 9x12" Sheet felt in a Vibrant Color

Yarn in the desired color(s)

Maker of Pom Poms

Needle for Embroidery

Thread for Embroidery

Stuffing

Directional Steps:

1. To make a pattern, cut out a stocking form from the paper/paper bag. It should be 1/2" larger on all sides than the finished stocking. If you like, you can look up patterns online. I just drew mine freehand!

2. Cut out four stocking forms from felt using the template (two for the outside, two for the lining). Make a 2" by 8" rectangle as well. Set aside two stocking pieces and the rectangle.

3. The other two will make you feel! Place one stocking shop's top corner on top of the felting mat. Remove a little piece of red roving and place it on top of the stocking, where you want the first stripe to start. (If you want it to appear like mine, start at the very top!) Use your needle felting tool to repeatedly punch it into the roving. It will begin to "adhere" to the wool. That indicates it's effective! Repeat until nothing comes off when you scratch your nail along it. Then, add another piece of roving and repeat the process across and down the wool felt until you have the desired size stripe. Mine were each about 3" thick.

4. Repeat with a few more stripes along the stocking. You can see where the stocking's foot is; I did a few different variations, one with the stripe getting wider at one point and one with the stripe remaining approximately the same size.

5. Now, repeat the process with the second stocking form, making sure to feel the OPPOSITE side. As you work on this one, use the finished striped piece to measure each one so the stripes line up when stitched together. It may not be flawless, but that's okay!

6. Sew the striped sides of each stocking together with a 1/2" seam on your sewing machine. Of course, leave the top open! Make little clips into the inseam along the contour of the foot (it will help it lay flatter when turned). Flip the right side out.

7. Stitch your other two stocking pieces together as well, but leave a 4-5" opening on one side! This will be your silver lining!

8. Take the previously cut rectangle and fold it in half lengthwise. Stitch all the way down the side where the long edges meet with a 1/2" inseam. Flip the right side out. This is the loop from which your stocking will hang!

9. Leave the lining stocking with the wrong sides facing out and insert the striped stocking (right sides facing out) into the lining. Pin the loop you made between the two. It should be fastened on the stocking's rear (heel) side, as shown! Now pin the entire top together.

10. Sew a 1/2" inseam around the whole top.

11. Turn the entire stocking right side out through the hole you left in the lining. Then, using a slip stitch, close that opening (you may use a machine or hand stitch it! I normally stitch by hand.

12. Stuff the liner into the striped stocking and you're done! You've got a stocking!!!

13. To make the pom poms, use the pom pom machine as directed. For each stocking, I produced two different sizes. You'll hang your letter on the piece you used to tie the pom pom together later, so leave it long!

14 Cut out two identical letter forms from felt to produce the feeling letters.

15. Use a blanket stitch to hand sew the two together. Before you finish the last few stitches, stuff!

16. Thread a needle with a long strand of yarn from one of your pom poms and stitch through the top corner of your letter to attach. 17. Attach to your stocking's loop!

CHAPTER SEVEN

The fundamentals of needle felting

Needle felting is a technique that sounds far more difficult than it is and produces quite charming results.

What's not to love about this? You'll be on your way to creating lovely fuzzy critters or any other felted things you can think of with just a few basic tools and a simple needle felting for beginners guide. Here are all of the tools and tips you'll need to get started with needle felting.

Needless to say, you don't have to be a knitter to try needle felting. The crafts involve a variety of equipment and even different sorts of wool. However, if you already knit, consider needle felting to be another enjoyable activity you can do with wool.

What You Require

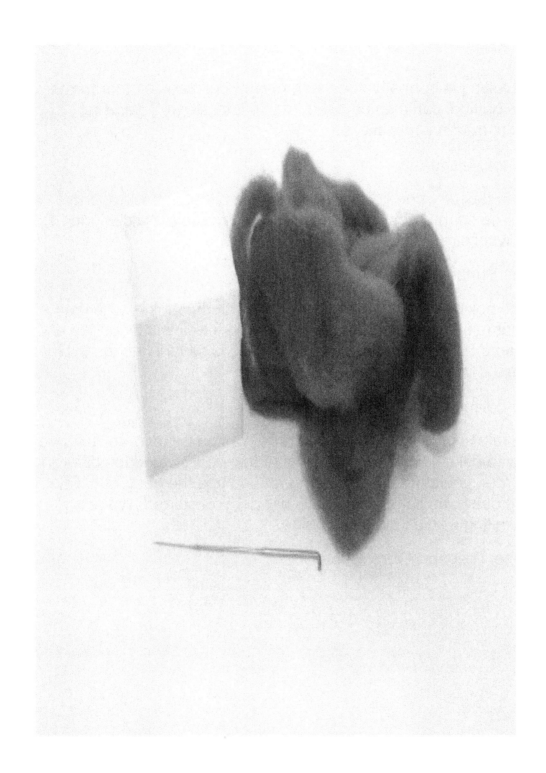

Wool

Needle felting is normally done with roving, but wool in other forms, such as batting, can also be used. In this tutorial, we'll be using roving cut from a larger piece.

Needle for Felting

It is not a tapestry needle or a sewing needle that you will use for felting. The sharp, barbed blades of a felting needle are designed to stir the wool strands.

A Felted Surface

To avoid poking your fingers, legs, or other body parts, you'll need a particular felting surface. Needle felting works well with sponges and foam pads. Simply ensure that your surface is several inches thick, such as the foam block in the image above.

Needle Felting Instructions

Needle felting processes vary depending on the project. You'll figure out how to poke your felting needle into the wool to produce different effects after you start experimenting and getting the hang of it. For the time being, these fundamentals will get you started. We're needle felting a little ball in this guide.

Step One: Prepare Your Wool

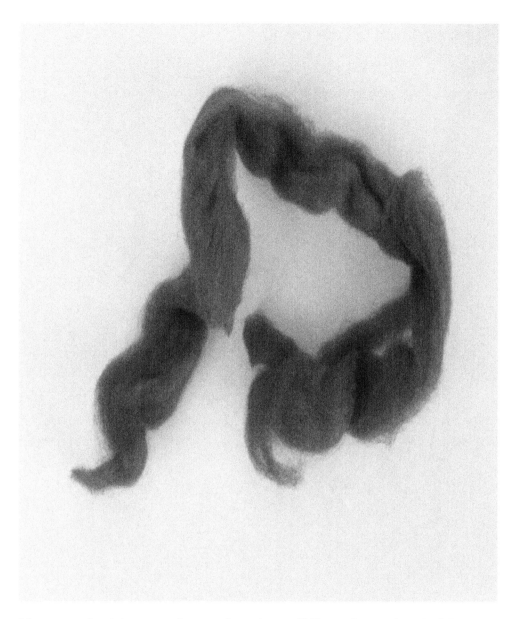

You can just tear a piece of roving off if you're using it. You don't have to cut it; the roving will readily pull apart on its own.

Step 2: Form a ball out of your roving.

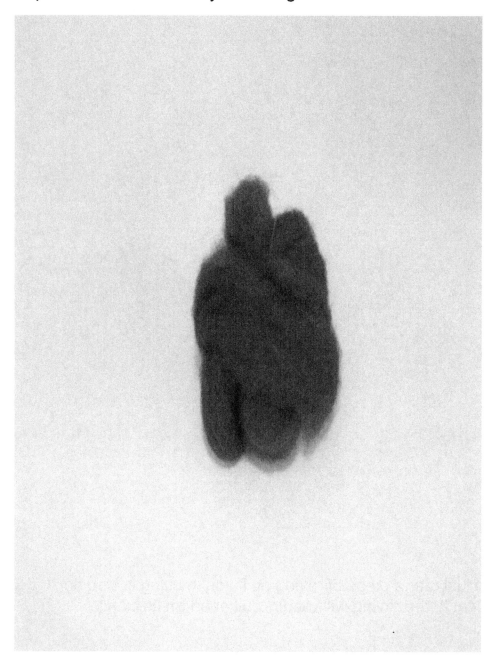

If at all possible, tuck the ends in.

Step 3: Make a poke with the ball.

To begin, place the ball on top of your felting surface. Then, with the needle, pierce the ball approximately 14-inch deep each time. Poke straight up and down so your needle may easily go in and out of the felt. Keep your fingers out of the needle's path. Felting needles are razor-sharp!

Step 4: Continue Until the Wool Felts

Continue poking the ball until the strands begin to link together and felt begins to develop. You'll likely notice that the ball has shrunk slightly.

What Can You Do With Needle Felting?

Animals are a favorite option among needle felters, and it's easy to see why: the felting needles produce a fuzzy appearance that resembles fur. However, you are not limited to making stand-alone animals or other items; you may also utilize a flat object, such as a scarf, as a base for your felted objects.

Try needle felting butterflies, flowers, or other ornaments directly onto the surface with a pair of mittens. (If you're going to needle feel onto a hand-knit item, make sure the gauge is tight so you have the nicest felting surface possible.) Alternatively, try needle felting a heart or similar form onto a plain sweater to add color. Needle felting can be used for more than simply decoration; it can also be used for mending. Is there a hole in your beloved sweater? To repair it, use needle felting!

What exactly are you waiting for? Grab your roving wool and a barbed needle, let your creativity run wild, and get felting!

Printed in Great Britain
by Amazon

38165155R00123